AMISH
CONFIDENTIAL

AMISH
CONFIDENTIAL

"Lebanon" Levi Stoltzfus
and Ellis Henican

G

Gallery Books

New York   London   Toronto   Sydney   New Delhi

G

Gallery Books
An Imprint of Simon & Schuster, Inc.
1230 Avenue of the Americas
New York, NY 10020

First Gallery Books hardcover edition March 2015

GALLERY BOOKS and colophon are registered trademarks of Simon & Schuster, Inc.

For information about special discounts for bulk purchases, please contact Simon & Schuster Special Sales at 1-866-506-1949 or business@simonandschuster.com.

The Simon & Schuster Speakers Bureau can bring authors to your live event. For more information or to book an event contact the Simon & Schuster Speakers Bureau at 1-866-248-3049 or visit our website at www.simonspeakers.com.

Interior design by Jaime Putorti

Manufactured in the United States of America

10 9 8 7 6 5 4 3 2 1

Library of Congress Cataloging-in-Publication Data

Stoltzfus, Levi.
 Amish Confidential / by Levi Stoltzfus and Ellis Henican. — First Gallery Books hardcover edition.
    pages cm
1. Stoltzfus, Levi. 2. Television personalities—United States—Biography. 3. Amish Mafia (Television program) I. Henican, Ellis. II. Title.
 PN1992.4.S79165A3 2015
 791.4302'8092—dc23
 [B]
                    2014047846

ISBN 978-1-5011-1030-6
ISBN 978-1-5011-1032-0 (ebook)

For my big brother Samuel Stoltzfus (1965–2013),
who was always there when we needed him most

CONTENTS

CONTENTS

PART III: BRINGING IT ALL BACK HOME

AMISH
CONFIDENTIAL

INTRODUCTION: PUBLIC ENEMY

What did I ever do to the governor? I had never even met the man. But the governor and his people had clearly been keeping a close eye on me. And now he had something important to reveal: Of all the thugs, criminals, miscreants and lowlifes in the state of Pennsylvania, I was Public Enemy Number One.

Me, a community-spirited businessman from a large Amish family! Me, a laid-back thirty-five-year-old who happened to appear in a popular television show! Apparently, the whole state—excuse me, the whole *country*—needed to be protected from me.

Okay, so maybe I'm not the perfect role model. I know some scruffy people. I do like to run around. When I was younger, I picked up a couple of DUIs, which I'm not proud of, okay? But other than those, the worst offense on my rap sheet is a measly dis-con, disorderly conduct, for mouthing off to a cop at the three-day Country Concert at Hickory Hill Lakes in Ohio. I wouldn't tell him where my tent was. I didn't want him watching me and my friends for the rest of our vacation. He found a nice holding cell for me instead. That might make me a bit of a hothead. It doesn't mean I'm a twenty-first-century Al Capone.

But there was Pennsylvania governor Tom Corbett in August of 2014, coming out of his hole in Harrisburg. His approval ratings were lower than poison ivy's. He was about as popular with the voters as deer ticks. And now he was aiming a fat load of phony outrage straight at me. What can I tell you? Politicians at election time will grasp at anything. Someone must have told the governor about *Amish Mafia*, the Discovery Channel series that follows my unlikely adventures as an unsanctioned guardian of the Amish. He must have taken me for the black-hatted John Gotti of south-central Pennsylvania. And now he was ready to pounce.

"Bigoted," Governor Corbett thundered.

"Negative, inaccurate and potentially damaging," he fumed.

"An affront to all people of faith," he roared.

The blustering governor signed a petition saying all of that and more. And he was demanding action, too. He wanted the TV show canceled. He wanted the sponsors to all pull out. He wanted the entire production, then entering its fourth successful season, packed up, shut down and bum-rushed out of the state.

Can you believe this guy? How did he get elected in the first place? Was he the governor of Pennsylvania or a frustrated TV critic? Didn't he have any real issues to worry about? If we were half as bad as he said we were, why had it taken him three years to speak up?

In the governor's hysterical view, our show was a stone-cold insult to the people of Lancaster County. "It changes the image of the county from one of pastoral beauty, where people are devoted to faith, family and friends," he contended, "to one of banal ugliness."

Banal ugliness. I wasn't even certain what that meant. But I was pretty sure it wasn't a compliment.

• • •

My name is Levi Stoltzfus, though most people know me as Lebanon Levi. Born and raised in a devout Amish family, I got tired of seeing Amish people pushed around by forces inside and outside the Amish community. I decided to do something that people from my background rarely do. I started speaking out and standing up. And I did it in public. I think everyone was surprised, me included, when our little TV show shot to the top of the Nielsen ratings, becoming the most watched show on the entire Discovery Channel. Suddenly, I was standing in the middle of this media tornado, semifamous, hugely controversial, wondering what exactly I had done to send the governor of Pennsylvania and his little lackeys around the bend.

I'll tell you what I did. I dared to start telling the truth about the Amish. The whole truth. The good *and* the bad. And that put a lot of people very much on edge. I went into the outside world, and I didn't slavishly repeat the usual Amish propaganda from the Lancaster County Chamber of Commerce and Pennsylvania Dutch Convention & Visitors Bureau. You know the stuff I mean: the saintly country bumpkins driving their buggies, milking their cows and hiding their faces from photographs. That version is fine as far it goes. Some of it is even true. But it's only a fraction of a much larger story, a small fraction. The rest of the story has been carefully hidden from most outsiders, and really it's the most interesting part. I had the nerve to go on television and start telling the rest.

The Amish are wonderful people. Don't get me wrong. I love the Amish. My family has been Amish for centuries. The Amish have made me what I am today. But the Amish aren't perfect. Nobody is. Not even me. The Amish are living, breathing human beings, not some tourist-brochure cartoons. The Amish have good and bad inside them and plenty in between. I'm sorry, Governor Corbett, but it's disrespectful and dishonest and just plain dumb to run around pretending otherwise.

I'm not sure what the penalty is for truth-telling in Pennsylvania. But I don't believe it's mandatory silence. So I'm not planning on piping down any time soon.

As you might imagine, I wasn't brought up knowing much about Nielsen ratings, political protests or reality TV. We were the plain and simple people. When I was a boy, we weren't even allowed to have a radio—and that was the 1980s. But slowly we learned. My older brothers found a beat-up Panasonic AM/FM and hooked it up to a twelve-volt car battery. You should have heard that sucker wail! They put it in the back of the family buggy and cruised Lancaster County on Saturday nights like they were the Amish reincarnation of the Beach Boys. My parents were from a different generation and a different mind-set. One night, my brother Henry got home late and forgot to haul the radio up to his room. My stepfather found the forbidden device as he was leaving for church the next morning. He didn't say anything to anyone. He just smashed the radio into many pieces in front of our house.

Message delivered. Message received.

But the lesson my older brothers learned from that wasn't the one my stepdad intended. Henry, Sam and Christian quit wasting time on battery-powered radios. They went looking for a small TV.

What can I say? Teenagers are teenagers everywhere, whether they're wearing black hats and suspenders or backward baseball caps and board shorts. Those Stoltzfus boys sure had spirit, you had to admit that.

Governor Corbett was half-right. The Amish are hardworking, God fearing, plain living, self-effacing, community oriented, suspicious of modern conveniences and all of that. But that's not all they are. There's a whole lot more to the Amish than that. There are Amish who go to the movies (I've loved action-adventure films since I was a teenager), drink alcohol (I'm a Captain Morgan–and–Sprite man), play in loud rock bands (bass guitar for me), follow the NFL (E-A-G-L-E-S, Eagles!), squabble with the neighbors, complain about the relatives, talk on cell phones, trade half-true gossip, judge one another harshly and flirt with the opposite sex—just like regular people do. Well, not *just* like regular people. In Amish Country, folks have their own unique ways of doing almost everything. Often, technicalities are cited. ("I only use the phone for business." "I'm spying on my neighbors to protect my kids.") Frequently, secrecy is involved. ("Why do you think God made tinted windows? So Amish drivers can relax at the red light!") Sometimes, the rules make no sense at all. ("Snaps are forbidden, pins are fine." "Electricity is the devil's juice, diesel's okay.") And it isn't just the laws of man the Amish have to worry about. Eternal damnation is an even bigger threat. From what I've heard, there's no time off for good behavior down there.

And yet these very same people are every good thing you've heard they are and more. The Amish are capable of extraordinary acts of kindness, forgiveness and decency. They'll rebuild a neighbor's barn after a fire. They'll give food and shelter to a struggling local family without expecting any payback. They'll go so far as to forgive a non-Amish milk-truck driver who commits mass murder inside a defenseless Amish school.

That, right there, in the space between the two extremes of Amish living, is where many real Amish people are today, the younger generation especially. Pulled between the ancient and modern, a foot in either world, new opportunities colliding with centuries-old guilt. Generations are changing. Time is marching on. The farms are worth millions. The children are harder to control. And Old Order Amish families are still riding around in horse-and-buggies—at least some of the time.

What the heck is going on here? People deserve answers. Real answers. That's why I decided to write this book.

We've addressed some of this on the TV show, far more than anyone ever expected us to. But there is so much more to tell. About the way the Amish treat one another when no one else is looking. About the bullying, the deceit, the conniving and the gossip. About the kindness and the generosity, too. About the face the Amish show to outsiders and the face they show to one another. Some days, it's a wonder those two faces even recognize each other.

The bishops won't discuss it. The visitors bureau won't, either. The professors and the pseudo-experts certainly won't, if they even know it, which many of them do not. Do you hear me, Professor Kraybill, with your rose-colored pronouncements about the Amish? Do you hear me, Mary Haverstick, with your petitions to yank my show? Do you hear me, Governor Corbett, with your cheesy Amish pandering at election time?

When you get right down to it, the Amish are a whole lot different from the fairy tale the world's been fed over the years. But read on. The rest of the truth is ahead.

You may be wondering how I can speak so freely about a society so closed. I will explain. My family connections and the power of the TV show give me some protection. But I draw even more from a technicality in the Ordnung, the code of conduct that all Amish people are expected to live by. Despite my solid Amish upbringing and my strong Amish roots, I had an eye-opening Rumspringa, the period when Amish teens get their first taste of real-world freedom. And I ultimately chose not to get baptized in the Old Order Amish church. I'm New Order Amish now, which is still pretty Amish. But there's enough wiggle room between the two to drive a black Cadillac through. Believe me, my current car has a much smoother ride than my old horse-and-buggy.

My traditional upbringing and my loving family taught me almost everything there is to know about being Amish. And for better or worse, this edgy TV show has turned me into the most famous Amish tough guy ever born. It's handed me a powerful platform, and I intend to keep using it. I have decided to take that special role of mine somewhere no Amish insider has ever gone before. Wish me luck. I'm going to need it.

I'm taking my marching orders from a higher authority, which is exactly what the Amish are taught to do. John 8:32: "And you will know the truth, and that truth will set you free." Not the tourist version. Not a bunch of misty-eyed Amish clichés. Not the random imaginings of some dimwitted politicians or clueless outsider or pseudo-experts. The truth. This is my real-deal, up-close-and-personal account of what it means to be Amish today. The inspirations and the contradictions. The soaring theory and the gritty practice. The many, many Amish realities that outsiders aren't supposed to see. This is what goes on behind the buggies, the bonnets and the beards.

So here's my tell-all tour of real Amish life, the way I have lived it and witnessed it over the past thirty-five years. It's an important story and a surprising one. I can promise you this much: Keep on reading, and you will never see the Amish the same way again. Hold on tight, now. The ride might be bumpy. But the fun has only begun. There is nothing plain and simple about the "plain and simple life."

PART 1
BEATING
MY PATH

CHAPTER 1
BECOMING US

You can't get much more Amish than we were.

When the actress Kelly McGillis was preparing for her role as a widowed Amish mother in the 1985 movie *Witness* with Harrison Ford, she moved into our house. She slept in the guest bedroom. She got up at four in the morning and had my brothers teach her to milk cows. "This is when I'm used to going to bed," she said, laughing. She planted rows of potatoes by hand but had trouble keeping the rows straight. She stared for hours at my mother, herself an Amish widow, mimicking my mom's hand gestures, learning her recipes, trying to get the Pennsylvania Dutch accent just right. That last one took some effort, but Kelly really nailed it. The boy in the film is called Samuel, my oldest brother's name.

When it came to being Amish, no one doubted the Stoltzfuses. Of course, we didn't think we were special. Most of the people we knew were just about like we were.

When I was little, we lived on a farm outside Quarryville in rural Lancaster County. That's in south-central Pennsylvania, the very heart of Amish Country. We spoke a language called Pennsylvania

Dutch, which isn't Dutch at all. It has nothing to do with Holland or wooden shoes or legal pot in Amsterdam. Pennsylvania Dutch is actually a kind of German—or "*Deutsch*," as the Germans say it, which the Americans heard as "Dutch," thereby confusing generations of baffled Amish Country tourists. To this day, they still show up in Lebanon County, Pennsylvania, and Holmes County, Ohio, and other Amish strongholds, and ask: "Where are the tulips and the windmills?"

On the farm, we grew corn and tobacco and raised dairy cows. My brothers and sisters and I were strictly forbidden to look at television, play video games or even listen to the radio. In fact, we had no electricity. Eating homemade ice cream after supper or reading Bible stories by kerosene lamp—that's what passed for prime-time entertainment at our house. School, we knew, would end for each of us after eighth grade, and that was totally legal under a special agreement the Amish have with Washington. In 1972, seven years before I was born, the United States Supreme Court said that the freedom of religion enjoyed by Amish families outweighed the state laws that kept most children in school until at least the age of sixteen. With that decision, the court ended for the foreseeable future any prospect of Amish doctors, Amish lawyers or Amish college professors. It also obliterated the whole concept of Amish high school and, with it, the possibility of ever hearing a bashful Amish homecoming queen say: "*Don't take my picture! I'm wearing a very, very plain dress!*"

We were Old Order Amish, the most traditional kind. We had running water and a diesel tractor, but we didn't have a telephone. If we had to make a call in an emergency, we went to a neighbor's house. And we didn't have a car. If somewhere was too far to walk, we rode in a black, horse-drawn buggy, which averaged five miles and one bucket of oats per hour. Our version of stepping on the gas was yelling at the horse.

From the time I could walk, my parents dressed me in a black hat, black pants, black suspenders and a plain white shirt with hand-sewn buttons. I dreamed of having snaps. God, I wanted snaps! But snaps were considered too fancy in an Amish family as plain as ours was, same as barbershop haircuts. We were strictly bowl-and-scissors kids. When the tourists stared at us or tried to take our pictures, we were taught to turn our heads away and look down.

Like many Amish families, our heritage went back into the mists of Switzerland in the fifteenth and sixteenth centuries. In those ancient days, a fiery group of students in Zurich had grown incensed that the Protestant Reformation was taking so long. It's a story I've heard my whole life. These young Swiss students thought Martin Luther, John Calvin and the other "reformers" had done a solid job slamming the corrupt practices of the Catholic Church, but where was the actual reform?

These complaints were not appreciated by Europe's Protestant leaders or the monarchs they loyally supported. The authorities arrested the young rabble-rousers, jailed them, tortured them, drowned them and warned everyone else not to be like them. The critics did what they could to survive. They hid out, fled the cities, abandoned their various trades and moved to the sparsely populated Low Country near the Swiss-German border, where they cultivated small farms. To them, big cities, big government, big religion and new technology represented nothing but threat and danger, and they and their followers would carry this suspicion of modern life for centuries to come. They wanted to worship in their own way and mainly to be left alone.

They called their faith Anabaptism, and they followed it fervently.

Unlike many other Christians, who baptized their children soon after birth, the Anabaptists declared their faith in the Lord when they reached adulthood. In fact, that's what *Anabaptist* means— "rebaptized" or "baptized again." Infant baptism didn't make sense, they believed, since a little child can't possibly understand the real meaning of good and evil. "Believer's baptism" was just one of many practices that set the Anabaptists apart from more conventional Christians.

The Anabaptists of Switzerland and Germany led very tough lives. The farm work was backbreaking. The winters were harsh. The local Catholics and Lutherans had absolutely no use for them. Life pretty much sucked all around. And their religion asked a lot of them. The Anabaptists had rules. Many, many rules. Rules about who they could marry (only each other). Rules about how they should pray (frequently, piously and not just at church). Rules about how to speak (softly) and how to have fun (hardly at all). They had rules for almost everything. With all their rules, the Anabaptists made the rigid German Catholics, who hadn't yet discovered guitar Masses or started calling the priests "Father Günther" and "Father Hans," seem loosey-goosey by comparison. Even though everyone prayed to the same Jesus, the Anabaptists knew Him as a score-keeping God, someone who demanded constant proof of moral righteousness. This was sackcloth-and-ashes Christianity with some hellfire and brimstone on the side. Heaven was up, and hell was down—with a very slippery slope in between.

Despite their move to the country, the Anabaptists were still being tormented by their old oppressors. The local authorities looked at the Anabaptists and thought: "Now, those are some people who are just begging for more persecution!" And so they got it. In 1526, the Zurich Council declared rebaptism punishable by drowning. "The third baptism," the punishment would come to be known as. That next year, Felix Manz, cofounder of the original Swiss Brethren congregation, became the first Anabaptist martyr. Four months later, Michael Sattler, a former Benedictine monk who'd become an Anabaptist leader, was executed by Roman Catholic authorities for the crime of heresy. His sentence read: "Michael Sattler shall be committed to the executioner. The latter shall take him to the square and there first cut out his tongue, and then forge him fast to a wagon and there with glowing iron tongs twice tear pieces from his body, then on the way to the site of execution five times more as above and then burn his body to powder as an arch-heretic."

The Anabaptists were easy targets. They were dedicated pacifists. They actually believed the line in the Bible that said to "turn the other cheek." Also there weren't too many of them, and in their rugged isolation, they always seemed a little strange. England's Edward VI and Elizabeth I were especially ardent persecutors, as was Spain's King Ferdinand, who famously said that drowning was "the best antidote to Anabaptism."

And just when things couldn't get any worse for the battered Anabaptists—well, they did. They had their very own schism. Now it wasn't just the other Christian denominations they were fighting with. They were also squabbling among themselves over just how strict their religion should be. The more tolerant Anabaptists, influenced by the theologian Menno Simons, became known as Mennonites. They didn't believe that every single word in the Bible had to be taken literally. Some parts, they thought, were more for general guidance. That sounded like blasphemy to the stricter Anabaptists, who followed the teachings of a stern-faced Jakob Ammann. He preached that true believers needed to "conform to the teachings of Christ and His apostles." Ammann was dissatisfied with what he saw as a loosening of rules and an acceptance of things too modern. He believed in stricter and longer church discipline and thought the Mennonites had gone recklessly soft.

"Forsake the world," he told his followers, who came to be known as the Amish.

Like his grandfather Ulrich and father, Michael, Jakob was a tailor. All the Ammanns were a little fixated on clothing. Jakob noticed that what a man wore was a good way to identify how successful he was. He also noted that stylish clothing allowed an individual to stand out. That's when he decided that his followers should always dress as plainly as they possibly could.

The Mennonites and Amish had much in common, but it was the narrow differences that everyone seemed to focus on. Jakob Ammann was a big believer in excommunication for anyone who didn't strictly follow the Bible's teachings, as interpreted by him, of course. The two groups also took sides over communion and foot washing. These were not gentle doctrinal discussions among people of largely similar beliefs. Anger ran hot and feelings were hurt.

Things in Europe didn't get any better for the Anabaptists. The grinding poverty, the relentless persecution, the internal strife—actually, it's amazing they lasted so long. Some Anabaptists tried moving to other parts of the continent, and the hostility followed them there. Things couldn't go on like this forever.

Finally, many of them had had enough. In the late 1700s and early 1800s, they pulled up stakes in Europe. A massive wave of Anabaptists collected their meager belongings and set sail for America, that famous place of religious liberty. That promised land of possibility. That growing, young country far, far away. They had the dream that other pilgrims had. Anabaptists settled first in south central Pennsylvania, in the rolling fields of Lancaster County, where the land was plentiful and comparatively fertile—and there was no one in the neighborhood hell-bent on persecuting them. The other local farmers were busy enough raising their own crops. There were plenty of strange people already in America. As different as the Amish were, they blended without much fuss into the patchwork of new settlers.

Lancaster wasn't the most obvious place to settle. It was a two-day buggy ride from New York or Philadelphia. But that was actually a plus for people who wanted a little distance between their new homes and anything "modern" or "worldly." Compared to the rigors of the Swiss-German border region, America appeared blessedly hospitable to them. They could live and farm and worship as they wanted, while mostly being left alone.

Far more smoothly than they expected, the Amish newcomers began putting down roots in their adopted homeland. They built farmhouses, tilled the fertile land, and got busy having children. They avoided going into town. They didn't build churches, not the physical kind. They didn't believe special buildings were required to worship. They gathered in small congregations and held services every other Sunday—rather than every week—in one another's homes. Each one of these congregations, twenty or thirty people, was its own Amish church.

Quickly, some of them found the scattered settlements of Lancaster County a little close for comfort. They hadn't come all the way to America to live on top of one another. Some Amish families migrated to eastern Ohio, settling on land that was deeded to them by President Thomas Jefferson. Others pressed into Indiana and beyond. And so the Amish fanned across the American countryside, finding new places where they could farm, live and worship as they chose.

They were deeply suspicious of central church government, so they didn't have any. Europe had been choked with that sort of thing, and it hadn't worked well for the Amish. In the Anabaptist tradition, each small congregation was its own little universe, answerable to its own bishop, a couple of preachers, perhaps a deacon or two— and to God. This local bishop truly was the master of his own little domain. The bishop baptized and married church members, same as the bishops do today. He imposed church discipline. He ordained new ministers. He settled disputes. He upheld and interpreted the Ordnung.

Ah, yes, the Ordnung.

The word in German means "order," "discipline," "rule," "arrangement" or "system." The Ordnung is the set of rules, based on biblical teachings, that all baptized Amish are supposed to live by. Everything Amish traces back one way or the other to the Ordnung. Beards, marriage, divorce, shunning, pacifism, dressing plainly, avoiding modern technology—matters large and small, subtle and obvious, all reside somewhere in the Ordnung.

I say "somewhere" because the Ordnung can be maddeningly difficult to pin down.

It is said there are two Ordnungs—one that is written and one that is not. In all the years I've attended Amish church services, I have never once laid eyes on any written rules. And yet they define the very essence of Amish life. It's the bishop's job to declare what the Ordnung says and means. This is where the bishops get a lot of their power.

Each local bishop gets to decide how the Ordnung applies to the issues of his congregation. He gets to decide when rules might have to change. He gets to decide who gets shunned and who doesn't. He gets to decide whose clothing is plain enough and which colors are allowed. He gets to decide who can have a telephone or a television or an automobile and who cannot.

Believe me, the list goes on.

It's an awful lot of power in the hands of one individual. But that's what it means to interpret the Ordnung. And often the bishops don't even agree among themselves, though they share the same core principles. Some are stricter than others. Some are quicker to change. Some consult closely with their congregations. Others are dictators.

In a way, this whole mixed-up scenario is perfectly suited for the Amish in America. Yes, we are deeply wedded to our rules and traditions. But didn't we travel across the ocean to the land of the free?

CHAPTER 2
HARD LESSONS

I wasn't born in a barn or a buggy or on my family's back porch. I arrived on June 30, 1979, at Lancaster General Hospital in a gleaming delivery room. Despite our famous suspicion of modern advances, Amish people go to doctors and hospitals like other people do. For reasons I've never been sure of, medical technology is almost entirely exempt from Amish disapproval. I was the seventh child of Mary and Eli Stoltzfus. I had three brothers and three sisters—Mary, Christian, Sadie, Henry, Samuel and Katie—who ranged in age from two to fifteen when I was born. And I was the tie-breaker. My mother had her first three children at home with a midwife, then went to the hospital for the rest. "Both are fine, but home was cheaper" was all my mother would say about that. Amish women are taught to always try to save money and never, ever make a fuss.

My full Christian name is Levi King Stoltzfus, though when I was little, I didn't feel like the king of anything. No Amish boy does. I had to listen to my parents, to my teachers, to my older brothers and sisters, to my aunts and my uncles, to the neighbors, to the other adults in our community, to the deacons, to the preachers, to the bishop—I'm sure I've forgotten a few of the other people I was supposed to listen to. But I remember this much: All of them spoke to me as if every syllable that flew from their mouths was the handed-down, sacred word of God. You get used to that when you grow up Amish. People are always telling you what to do and how to do it and acting like Moses just handed them the tablets.

I'm still looking for the place in the Bible where it says you aren't allowed to listen to the radio or ride in a car or go to a barbershop and get a haircut that isn't shaped like a porridge bowl. I haven't found it yet, but I'm still looking. It's got to be in there somewhere, since so many people I know believe it so fervently!

The "Levi" part of my name comes from the Old Testament, like a lot of Amish names do. It's right up there in Amish popularity with Eli and Jacob and Amos, or Sarah and Esther for a girl. In any Amish schoolroom, there will almost always be two or three Levis and no Justins or Taylors or Brittneys. I was Levi S. to my teachers long before I was Lebanon Levi to my friends. In the Bible, Levi is the third of Jacob's twelve sons. The name means "attached" or "joined" in Hebrew. I guess they give you that name so you won't get too many ideas about straying off as an individual and forgetting the group.

I always liked stories. When I was young I wasn't allowed to see movies like *Terminator* or *Die Hard*, but I had plenty of Bible stories, the wilder and bloodier the better, as far as I was concerned. Levi's descendants became the priests of the Israelites. It's all laid out in Genesis 34. When his sister Dinah is raped by Shechem the Hivite—now *there's* a frightening name—Levi seeks revenge, resulting in his tribe, the Levites, losing all their property. This seemed terrible but it turned out to be fortunate. When the

Assyrians deported and effectively destroyed most of the Israelite tribes, the landless Levites found refuge with the powerful tribe of Judah—and survived.

Go, Levites!

I have a few dim memories of my very early years. Clomping across the grass outside our farmhouse when I'd just learned to walk. Bumping against the hay bales in the barn. My mother cooking dinner, my father sitting in his chair, my brothers and sisters chasing each other around the house while I sat on the floor in the living room playing with my little carved wooden toys. My favorites were the ones that were shaped like cows, sheep, horses and any other animals.

I loved my father. He was a large man with big hands and large shoulders. He liked to have fun with his brothers, and he talked in a loud voice. He worked very hard on the farm. According to my mother, when I was really little, I liked to sit next to him while he ate. I'd put my little feet in his lap. "That's the only way you would eat good," my mother told me, "sitting right next to your father like that."

I don't really remember that, but I'm sure it's true.

The last memory I have of my father is a September morning in 1981. I was two years old. He'd been out in the fields, early as usual, and had just come back in for a quick breakfast. Since he was just going to be inside for a few minutes, he left his hat on. He sat in the chair where he usually sat, and I climbed into his lap. I remember all of this like it was yesterday. I remember exactly how he looked that morning. I remember how he smelled like fresh-cut grass. I remember him keeping his hat on.

I remember him hugging me as he got up from the chair and said good-bye.

He was working in the barn that day with my brother Henry, who was fourteen at the time. They were filling the silo with chopped-up corn for the livestock to eat. My father was standing next to the tractor, feeding corn onto the cutter's conveyor belt. As the corn was dumping in, the cutter got clogged somehow. My father reached to unclog it without turning the tractor off. Either he opened the cutter hood too quickly or the hood flew open—we never knew exactly. But somehow he got pulled into the cutter, where his leg was cut off clear up to the hip.

Henry didn't see it happen. But he certainly heard the grinding machinery and my father's bloodcurdling screams. My brother spun around immediately and frantically shut the tractor off. There was so much racket in the silo, my mother could hear it in the house. She grabbed me in her arms and we went running, while someone ran to the house of a neighbor, a non-Amish neighbor with a telephone, to call an ambulance.

We all stood beside the tractor and the cutter and my dad, waiting for help to come from downtown Lancaster. It was less than half an hour, but my dad was bleeding hard on the silo floor. It felt like fifteen years. By the time they got him to the hospital and tried to stitch him up, my dad had lost too much blood. There was nothing the doctors could do to save him. He held on for four long days, and then he died.

The next thing I remember is when we were at the viewing, and all my uncles were really nice to me. I remember my aunts and all my cousins being there. I was so young, I didn't know what it meant exactly to have my father be dead.

There was a little stepstool, what we call a hassock, next to my father's coffin. I remember standing on my hassock. I reached in and combed his hair. Isn't it strange, the little details you remember from a time like that?

Three weeks later, my brother Henry burned the barn down.

It's crazy, but I think he might have blamed himself for my father being killed. The Amish didn't have anything like grief counseling back then. The neighbors did what the Amish do. They came right over and raised a new barn for us. I think it took two days.

Amish people are warm and generous that way, always ready to help a neighbor in need.

I was sad for a very long time. I didn't want to play with the other children. I stayed alone in my quiet little world, passing the hours on the living room floor with my hand-carved wooden animals. I had a tiny cow and a tiny sheep and a tiny goat and three tiny horses— perfect Amish toys. I would line them up in little rows, then knock them down with my hand. Somehow, this made me feel better. When I got tired of playing, I would put all the wooden animals into a wagon that I parked beside my mother's chair. When friends and neighbors came to visit and console my mother, they also brought new wooden animals for me. I took them and mumbled, "Thank you," barely looking up from the floor.

The hours stretched on like days. I can only imagine how my mother and my older brothers and sisters felt. It would take a couple of years before I was totally comfortable leaving my mother's side.

My two oldest brothers, Sam and Henry, were a tremendous help to me. They were out of school already and stayed busy on the farm. Sam, who was sixteen at the time, was like a dad to me. He took me with him when he went places. He would always buy me candy. He wasn't married yet, and he treated me like a son.

My uncles came around a lot, my father's and my mother's brothers, making a genuine effort to look after us. They inquired about the farm work and constantly asked my mother if she needed anything. My uncle Eli Ebersole let me sit with him at church on Sunday so I wouldn't always have to sit with my mother. Little boys sat with their mothers in the women's pews, but older boys got to sit with the men.

Slowly, I came out of my shell. Uncle Eli told me I was a lot like my father. "You're active," he said. "You're talkative. I like seeing you happy." I'm not sure if he was exaggerating—I know I didn't feel too happy—or if he was just giving me a name to live up to. But eventually, life started feeling more normal.

Some people said I looked like my father, but I didn't really know. With the Amish ban on photography, I was working only from memory. To this day, I still wonder what my father would be like, what we would be doing together, where I'd be living, and how I would have grown up differently. As a child, you can't lose a father like that and not have it affect everything.

An Amish widow doesn't have a lot of dating opportunities, especially not back then. To be fair about it, neither does an Amish widower.

After my father died, you can imagine how busy my mother's life became, and it wasn't like she was just sitting around before. Now she was doing everything she and my father had done together, but she was doing it alone. Keeping the farm running, raising seven children as well as she could, doing it all with hardly any modern conveniences. Sure, my uncles and my brothers pitched in, but that wasn't the same as having a husband, especially one as vibrant and energetic and competent as my dad.

Without a car, she couldn't travel far. With all those needy children and animals, she couldn't be out long. And she was a decade or two older than most of the other single people who were Amish. By and large, the Amish marry early. They're out of school in eighth grade. They aren't supposed to have premarital sex. What's there to do but get married? That's what many conclude. So for a woman my mother's age, there weren't too many prospects around. About the only places she ever went were to church and to the store sometimes, and to see the relatives, who all lived a short buggy ride away.

Really, who was my widowed mother going to meet?

But my mom wasn't the first Amish woman to lose her husband, and it turned out that the Amish had a system for situations like hers. The Amish have systems for a lot of things. This one had several moving parts.

Friends introduced other friends. Widows and widowers wrote letters back and forth. Occasionally, two people would meet at church. But those were all hit-or-miss possibilities. You couldn't really count on any of them. So the visiting began.

Someone would get a bunch of widows together with a bunch of widowers. They'd go and visit one another's houses. It was like group dating—group visiting, really, since the conversations weren't known for being romantic. They'd bring food along, and people would sit and talk.

It was at one of those group visits that my mother met an Amish deacon from Lebanon County, about an hour's buggy ride from her farm in Lancaster County. He came to visit her house with a group. Later, she and a group visited his home. His name was David Peachey. Like my mother, he came from a well-known Amish family. Like my mother, he had a happy life that was marked by sudden tragedy.

On September 20, 1984, three years after my father died, he had been out for a ride with members of his family. His wife, Melinda, was with him in the buggy. So were two of the couple's nine children, Nancy, twenty-three, and Esther, age seven. They were on Route 419 about a quarter mile south of Newmanstown in Lebanon County. That's not a very busy road.

They had no idea what hit them.

A pickup truck, driven by a man the authorities said had been drinking, slammed into the back of the Peachey family buggy. According to the felony criminal complaint, Jeffrey Linnette of Newmanstown kept driving after crashing into the buggy, then pulled over and got out of the truck and ran away.

The buggy was totaled. The mother and the older daughter were killed. The father and the younger girl were badly hurt, but their injuries weren't life-threatening. And the Pennsylvania state police put out word from the Jonestown Barracks to area hospitals, asking that everyone be on the lookout for an accident victim seeking treatment. When Linnette arrived at Reading Hospital with multiple cuts and a broken nose, the hospital staff quickly called the police.

It took a while for the case to wind its way through the state courts of Pennsylvania. Ultimately, Linnette pled guilty to two counts of murder by vehicle and several other charges and headed off to prison.

•   •   •

It's hard to say exactly what drew the two of them together. I never asked, and they never volunteered. Was it the loneliness, the day-to-day hardship or the tragedy they obviously shared? Or was it just a lucky connection? Whatever it was, Deacon David Peachey and my mother, Mary, courted Amish-style. That meant additional visits to each other's houses—eventually without the rolling widow-and-widower brigade. And I consider all of us blessed by what happened next. The two of them, David and Mary, married, and my mother's new husband became my stepfather, the man who would truly raise me. From that day forward, I thought of him as and called him my father. His seven children became my stepbrothers and -sisters, and I am so grateful to have them in my life. We moved to his farm in Lebanon County, which was plainer and more rudimentary than ours in Lancaster County had been. When we moved to Lebanon County, I had to leave my friends behind. I had to go to a new one-room Amish school. I wasn't upset about any of that. I was just thrilled to have a new dad. I didn't really think of him as my stepdad. From the day he and my mother got married, he just became my dad. With our two families blended together, I guess you could say we were like the Amish *Brady Bunch*, though since we had no television, we had no idea who those people were. And there were way more of us.

All together, my mom and stepdad had fifteen children, though Sam and Henry were around only some of the time and Katie, my oldest sister, got married around the same time my mother did. My oldest stepsister was also married. So we really only had ten or eleven children around the new house most nights. I say "only," but it was still a lot of kids.

We all got along right away. There was a big, long table where we'd all sit down to eat. The new house was a joyful place to be. I know it was tough for my new father. He had a lot of mouths to feed. But he never complained about anything. That's how it was. We lived off the land. We had a big garden. And that's how we survived. We'd butcher a steer and a couple of pigs every fall and then we were set for the winter. We had steaks and pork chops and bought some items at the store—but not too much. Mom did a lot of canning, which made the food taste better than freezing it. All considered, we ate really well.

We didn't live like cavemen. Like most Amish families of the era, we had some semimodern conveniences. We just didn't push it too far. In the living areas, we had kerosene lights. In the bedrooms, it was strictly candles and oil lamps. A wick drew up the oil, and that's how we could see at night. It's a little brighter than a candle, and that's what we used to read.

We had diesel engines to run the milking machine and tractor. We ran our water with an air-pressure pump. My mother cooked with propane, and the refrigerators ran off propane, too. But the big deep-freezer needed electricity. To skirt the prohibition, we paid rent to keep a freezer over at a non-Amish neighbor's house. We'd chop up some meat and freeze some sweet corn and keep it over there through the long Pennsylvania winters.

Even in winter, it wasn't cold in the house. We had some wood fires but mostly we used coal. The coal burned longer and hotter. We had little vents going up the wall to the ceiling so the heat would rise upstairs. Still, upstairs was always a little colder. My parents' room was downstairs. The kids' rooms were on the second level. I shared a bed with my brother Chris. There was another bed in the room that Sam and Henry slept in when they were at home. My three stepbrothers slept in another room—two double beds and a single. Same with the girls. They had two beds and four girls in a room.

Today, this sounds almost crazy. But when I was growing up, I couldn't imagine living any other way. What else did we know? We didn't live any differently from most of our Amish relatives, neighbors and friends. Mostly, I remember it as fun.

CHAPTER 3
LEARNING ENGLISH

When I was little, we didn't know many English.

The English—that's what the Amish call anyone who isn't Amish—could be young or old, black or white, native-born or immigrant. They could speak Spanish, Urdu or Swahili. To us, all of them were "English." When your first language is Pennsylvania Dutch, which isn't really Dutch but German, and most of the outsiders you encounter are prattling away in English, it's no wonder that word has no particular connection to London, Oxford or Manchester.

It just means "not us."

I wasn't taught to fear the English, and it wasn't until later that I started envying some of the cool toys they had. When I was growing up, the English just didn't seem that relevant to our lives. They were the tourists who stared at us when we took the buggy into town. They were the people who lived down the road. We didn't really *know* them. They lived their lives, we lived ours. We didn't ask much from them or they from us. Mostly, we just wanted the English to leave us alone, and that seemed okay with them. My family, many of our neighbors, all of our friends—everyone I was close to was Old

Order Amish. If they weren't official members of an Amish church, they were at least defined in Amish terms: ex-Amish, shunned Amish, raised by Amish or, God willing, coming back into the holy fold sometime soon.

We knew a few of our English neighbors. The Bohns. The Hoffmans. The Crouses. They were pleasant enough when you'd see them. They were happy to make little arrangements with us, especially when small cash payments were involved. We borrowed an English family's telephone. We rented space in their garage for our freezer. We'd lend an occasional hand on their farms whenever they asked us to. But we didn't hang out with them. Their kids weren't coming over for playdates. The adults weren't dropping by each other's houses with fresh-baked bread. If they looked at us as odd though mostly harmless creatures, that's about how we looked at them.

The only real sour note was our worry that, not being Amish, the English people might have trouble getting into heaven. That wasn't something we mentioned to them. That would have been rude. But whenever we thought about it, it made us feel sorry for them. They might have had all manner of modern conveniences and labor-saving devices in their houses. But all those gadgets, we feared, would be mighty cold comfort in the face of eternal damnation.

Eventually, some cracks began to appear in this sealed-off existence of ours. It was the Amish girls who usually got the first look inside the exotic, foreign world of the English, so different from the way we were living and yet right down the road from us. When my sisters and stepsisters got done with eighth grade, they started picking up part-time work cleaning English peoples' houses. They earned minimum wage or slightly better. You wouldn't call the work glamorous, but it was all indoors. It was definitely easier than bundling hay or carrying milk buckets. And it had an additional benefit: Once those Amish girls got inside those English houses, they couldn't turn their heads away from modern American living. They even got some hands-on experience.

"Everything runs on electricity," my sister Sadie marveled, "even the door for the garage!"

"They have, like, three different machines just for cutting up food," my sister Mary said. "I don't even know why they need knives." Truly, the girls had not seen anything like that before.

These people's houses were stocked with every kind of appliance you could imagine. Sunbeam, Frigidaire, Kenmore—even the names sounded otherworldly to my sisters and their friends. In many cases, the young Amish housekeepers had no idea what these machines were for or exactly how to operate them. The English ladies had to teach their Amish housekeepers. What did these girls know about Waring blenders and something called a Cuisinart and modern washing machines? At home, our washing machine had two open tubs, a set of rollers to squeeze the water out and an air pump to bring fresh water in. The English people had Whirlpools with knobs and buttons and three different temperature settings—and electric clothes dryers, too. Some of these people had no clotheslines at all!

The learning curve was steep and sometimes rocky. One afternoon, my sister Sadie came home in tears. She'd had trouble with an Electrolux vacuum cleaner at work. Instead of adjusting the hose so the air would suck in, she had the air blowing out. I guess the woman walked in and saw Sadie standing in the living room with a baffled look on her face, blowing dirt and dust all over the first floor of the house. Sadie didn't know any better. At home we used a sturdy broom made of corn straw. She had never used a vacuum cleaner before. The woman exploded.

"What is wrong with you?" she demanded. "Do I have to hold your hand all day?" Sadie ran all the way home, saying she was never going back again.

Our dad had to go over and talk to the lady. I'm not sure exactly what he said, but he could be persuasive when he wanted to be. He managed to smooth things over, and Sadie went back to work.

She learned to vacuum. She also learned to appreciate the advantages of other labor-saving household appliances. It didn't escape her notice that she was using these magical machines to do her paid work, while she and her mother and sisters were toiling with hand mops and feather dusters at home.

"They have nice things," I remember Sadie saying after she'd been there awhile. She didn't actually say she might want some modern things of her own one day, but I could hear it in her voice.

At about the same time, my older brothers and sisters were reaching the age of Rumspringa, when young Amish are invited to get a taste of the outside world. Rumspringa begins at age sixteen and usually ends with a decision to get married.

Give my siblings credit. They took up the challenge valiantly. My brothers even more than my sisters, I would have to say. They weren't out robbing liquor stores or attending swingers' sex clubs (not that I know of, anyway), but given the place they and I had come from, they made some giant leaps. And they beat a path for me.

They learned to drive cars, though our dad would never let them park up at the house. They got their first radio—and when my dad busted the radio, their first TV. They sampled alcohol and maybe some other stuff, too. I was too young to do any of that. My brothers made at least some efforts to shield my tender ears, but I'd hear stuff.

This guy got drunk . . . This other guy kissed a certain girl. They tried not to talk too much in front of me. They probably didn't want to corrupt me too young. They also didn't want me telling our parents. But it's tough keeping secrets around any house, especially one as tightly packed as ours was.

One guy bought a car . . . Some girl was chasing after a certain guy. He kissed her when he wasn't supposed to . . . Someone's sister went out back and smoked a cigarette.

None of this behavior could be called genuinely bad. For English teenagers these were just normal rituals of youth. The lines for Amish teens, of course, were drawn a whole lot tighter. Scandal for us was weighed on a far more delicate scale.

"Jake went to a concert with other members of the church," my brother Chris announced one day, before quickly warning me not to say anything. I don't remember who the group was, but they weren't performing Christian hymns, I am sure.

The truth is, I wasn't naturally discreet. I was a talkative kid, and I would talk to anyone, including my parents. To Chris and Henry and Samuel and the others, a talkative younger sibling could be a dangerous thing. I didn't mean any harm by it, but I was always curious. I wanted to know what was going on, and my older brothers were probably right to be a little careful around me.

One day, we were all up at the Farm Show Complex in Harrisburg, showing some hogs we had raised. That was something we did every year, bringing our best livestock to the farm show. Other families brought their sheep or horses or cows. A lot of Amish women showed off their homemade pies. But this particular year, the Farm Show Complex also had the Monster Truck Spectacular going on at the same time. My twin stepbrothers, Daniel and Samuel, slipped away from the farm show and spent the afternoon with the world's largest and loudest trucks. I don't believe anyone told them not to—not in so many words. But I'm quite certain that had he been asked, Jakob Ammann would not have approved of monster trucks.

I heard my stepbrothers talking about it later. They thought the trucks were totally cool. And while they were missing in action from our family outing and admiring the huge machinery, they ran across two Amish sisters they knew. The girls must have been monster-truck fans, too—or at least fans of the boys who were monster-truck fans.

Without really thinking, I innocently mentioned to my dad that the twins said they ran into the sisters at the monster-truck show. I certainly didn't mean to get anyone in trouble, but boy, did I pack a lot of it into those few words!

My dad confronted my brothers. I'm not sure if he also told the girls' parents, but somehow they found out. All I know is that everyone was blaming me.

"I can't believe you told Dad!" Daniel yelled at me.

"We can't tell you anything!" Samuel said.

"Thanks a lot," one of the sisters told me when I saw her. "I hope you're happy with yourself. Now we'll never be able to go anywhere."

The Amish are touchy like that. I swear, I didn't even realize I was doing anything wrong.

As my parents often said: *"Kinner un Narre saage die Waahret"*— children and fools speak the truth. In hindsight, it makes me cringe.

Like it or not—and certainly our parents didn't—the outside world was leaking in. As far as my parents were concerned, the old ways had been good enough for their parents and their parents' parents and on back into history. Surely, those ways were good enough for us. For centuries, they had been good enough for the Amish. The teachers at school, the preachers at church, they constantly warned us to cast our gaze away from the temptations of the modern. That was fool's gold, they told us, shiny but worthless. Those fancy baubles would lead us all down terrible paths. But the nineteenth century, which was more or less the one we were living in, was inevitably giving way to the late twentieth, even as all the grown-ups around us insisted such a thing could never, ever be allowed.

It got me thinking, I'll tell you that.

I wondered why the Amish rules seemed to be applied so unequally. Why were some modern conveniences strictly forbidden and others not? An electric clothes dryer was the devil's contraption, but a gas-powered water heater was perfectly fine. One kind of tractor was acceptable, another kind was not. When I put my young mind to the subject, the list of contradictions never seemed to stop. If the outside world was so fraught with danger, why were we letting any of it in? And if it wasn't, why were the old people making such a fuss? Some modern conveniences were clearly welcome improvements. Why not others?

I thought a lot about telephones.

If telephones were so awful and we must never have a phone in our house, why was it okay to use a neighbor's phone when we wanted to?

The telephone thing really got me. I heard my father mention that several of his friends had installed telephones in their houses.

"How can they do that?" I asked my father.

"Well," he said, explaining as well as he could, "the phone is just for business. They need it for work."

But wait, wasn't the phone a bad thing? Didn't it sap our energy and steal our time? If it was okay to have a phone for business, why not for family things? None of this made any sense to me. To his credit, my dad didn't try to pretend that it did.

"That's just the interpretation," he said, shrugging.

I could think of other examples, lots of them. If electric freezers were such a terrible thing, why were we renting space to keep one at the neighbor's house? If we looked the other way when my older brothers were driving their evil cars, why did it matter where they parked?

For that matter, why was it that we couldn't drive a car if we could ride in one as long as it was driven by someone not Amish? What sense did that make?

The older I became, the more these contradictions got to me. I understood being religious and praying to God. If you're a Christian like I am and you believe in the Bible, you know that God made everything and everyone and dispatched his son down to earth. You know that heaven's up and hell is down and heaven's a whole lot nicer. That much was clear.

But the questions kept coming. Why did all that mean that our family had to live like it was 1830 all over again? Why not the 1950s or the Stone Age? Why horse-and-buggies? Why not high-fin Cadillacs or Fred Flintstone carts? Was it just because the 1800s were when many of our Anabaptist ancestors came from Europe to America with the words of Jakob Ammann ringing in their ears: "Forsake the world"?

Is that why we were stuck where we were—no TVs, no toasters, no video games, whatever those were? Not even man-powered, pedal-pushing bicycles?

Actually, yes. That pretty much summed up why we couldn't have those things. We didn't because they hadn't, and as far as the preachers were concerned, we probably never would.

The forebodings never stopped. If the Amish people ever got used to all those modern and just barely modern contraptions, we were warned, pretty soon we'd be worshiping stereo systems and central air-conditioning like everyone else did—instead of the Lord. Instead of paying attention to our families and the church, folks would be glued to televisions and jabbering away on telephones. Obviously, someone had this all figured out. All those labor-saving devices—in the kitchen and in the fields—would only make people believe they didn't need their families or the rest of the Amish community anymore. If a woman could make a cake batter with a mixer, she wouldn't need her daughter's help anymore, would she? If a man could use a giant tractor to plow his fields, his son could be off doing who knows what. And if everyone started driving cars and speeding all over creation, how would anyone keep the traditional family close by? Before you knew it, the Amish would be like everybody else.

For a while, explanations like those satisfied me. Kids know what they know, and I only knew being Amish. But as time went on, the questions got louder inside my head, and the answers got even harder to find.

CHAPTER 4
FREE AT LAST

I was dying to turn sixteen. I wouldn't have to wear a hat anymore.

It's funny, the things you focus on when you are young. For me, it was the hat—my big, black, full-brimmed, Amish hat. That hat sat so large on my head, sometimes I almost felt like I would disappear beneath it. I'd worn a hat since I was two years old. My mother attached a small tie that went under my chin to keep the hat from falling off when I ran around the yard. As a teenager, I didn't need the chin strap anymore, but the hat still felt like it was lashed onto my head. To me, that hat represented everything that frustrated me about being young and Amish, living under my parents' roof, being subject to all the Amish rules, whether those rules made any sense to me or not. God, I hated wearing that hat! Up until sixteen, I knew, the rule was: Wear your hat. I also knew that once I got to be an adult and I got baptized in the church as everyone just assumed I would—me included—then I'd have to wear a hat every day again. But there was this window, this little period of time, this very special moment. From sixteen, when I would start going to youth group, until whenever it was I finally got baptized—in my twenties, probably—I could run around anywhere I wanted without having to wear a hat. This represented freedom to me.

I had only the vaguest idea of what else freedom might mean. But I was pretty sure I knew how to spell it: R-U-M-S-P-R-I-N-G-A.

A quick word about the word: *Rumspringa* comes from German, as so much in Amish life does. That's why we pronounce the word *ROOM-shpring-ah*. But its history and meaning have been bent, chopped and twisted by the continents and the years. It all goes back to the German verb *herumspringen*—literally "to jump or hop around." Yes, it sounds like some of the parties I've been to, but there's more to it than that. Like a lot of long German words, *herumspringen* gets its meaning from its individual parts. In German, *her* means "here," and *um* means "about." So the first part of the word, *herum*, adds up to "hereabout."

Now the second part: *Springen* is a German word meaning "to jump" or "to skip." Simple enough, except that the Swiss came along and put their own spin on it. To them, *springen* also meant "to run." So to our Amish ancestors along the Swiss-German border, *rumspringen* was a verb meaning, more or less, "to run around."

To complicate matters just a little more, the word got changed again when the Amish brought it to America. This happened to a lot of words. In the case of *herumspringen,* the *he* was chopped off the front, leaving just the *rum,* and the *en* at the back of the word was shortened to an *a. Rumspringa* was used as a noun as well.

And there it stands, ready to signify an important time of Amish life: *Rumspringa*—a time for running around.

For the young Amish like me, it all begins at age sixteen. At sixteen, you get to join a youth group and go away on Sundays. "Gangs," these groups are sometimes called. Like, "What gang are you in?" They aren't criminals or anything like that. It's just a name, and you're expected to pick one. You're allowed to find a gang anywhere in the Amish community. It's your choice. It doesn't have to be in your church or your part of the county, and the groups have different personalities, from the plainest to the wildest.

In the plainer groups, the boys still choose to wear their hats and the girls always keep their bonnets on, even though they don't have to, and everyone rides in open buggies. Then there are groups that have some open buggies and some covered buggies. And there are groups that get a little wilder, riding in covered buggies and maybe even a car or two. Yes, that's what passes for semi-wild in Amish youth groups. There are also some youth groups with all cars where everybody's riding around like *The Fast and the Furious* or some undiscovered NASCAR team.

It's the same spread with haircuts—going from all bowl cuts to a mixture to all barbershop haircuts. The girls' hairstyles are also different from gang to gang. In some gangs, the girls still wear their hair hidden under bonnets. In others, the girls undo their braids and let their waist-length hair go flying in the breeze. There are groups who don't drink alcohol and groups who drink a little and groups where it seems like no one's ever sober. They're toasting everything except their next confession. It's up to the individual to choose.

Still, most kids do what I did. They start out with a youth group close to home, a group that their friends are part of. That's who they know so that's where they go. This is one of the first big decisions an Amish teenager gets to make. Officially, it's your choice, but choice is not something Amish kids have a lot of experience with. You didn't get to pick your church or its many, many rules. In school, there weren't any electives to choose from. You certainly didn't pick how to dress or which chores to do. Your parents made all those choices, under the strong influence of the church and the local bishop. So even if it's only "I'm going where Ruben and Isaac are going," for the first time ever, well, at least those words came out of your mouth.

I started out with a horse-and-buggy group in Lebanon County. They were so plain, they didn't even really have a name. Some of the other groups had names, like the Crickets, the Lightning and the Renegades. Also the Hurricanes, the Seahawks and—these weren't quite as wild sounding—the Swans and the Antiques. I also heard about some car-driving groups that called themselves the Avalanches, the Dominoes, the Checkers and—these sounded almost like real gangs—the Cougars and the Sharks.

The youth group I chose was just known as the Lebanon youth group. They had a couple of cars that they didn't use too often, and that was about it. They didn't go many places, and when they did, someone had a set of reins in his hands. Most of the kids in my Lebanon group didn't have haircuts, either. They do now, but they didn't back then. They didn't drink much. That might have made us popular with the parents, but it didn't make these kids very much fun to hang out with. After years of imagining the blowout I'd have when I finally turned sixteen, I probably came off as a little bit of a rebel, or at least impatient. I was one of the only kids who had a haircut and left his hat at home.

No one in the community had any reason to whisper about what went on with the Lebanon youth group. We got together on Sundays around four or five in the afternoon. We played volleyball and some other games, then we had a meal together, then everyone sang some Christian hymns, then we all went home.

Really, that was it.

As far as I was concerned, Rumspringa was starting out as a huge disappointment. I could have stayed at home and done most of that. The only difference I could see was that of all the boring things we were doing, some boring girls were doing them with us. During the week, I did my usual farm work. Every other Sunday, I went to church in the morning. This was my big excitement? After all the tales I'd heard from older kids, this wasn't my idea of Rumspringa at all. As far as I was concerned, I hadn't been waiting sixteen years for *this*. And the girls barely even talked to me. They just talked to one another.

I knew I had to find another group to Rumspringa with.

I still had a few friends from Lancaster County, kids who'd been there when I was a baby and some I knew through my brothers Christian and Henry, who'd never liked Lebanon County and went back to live with my Lancaster uncles as soon as they possibly could. If you live in a big city, Lancaster County, Pennsylvania, may not sound like a major metropolis. But compared to Lebanon County, believe me, it was Rome, Paris and New York rolled into one. Lancaster is the biggest area anywhere for the Amish community, especially Amish youth. All the other counties are smaller. When I was seventeen, I told the Lebanon group good-bye and switched to a youth group in Lancaster County.

That was more like it. Finally, the only times I was expected to wear a hat were when I went to church and to funerals.

My new gang was called the Souvenirs. I liked the way that sounded immediately. It was from those guys that I got the nickname I still carry around, Lebanon Levi. I was the guy from Lebanon County. They had so many Levis and Johns and Rubens, they needed some way to tell everyone apart. If you're John from Perry County, you're Perry John. As soon as I got there, I was Lebanon Levi. Everything was faster in Lancaster, including the nicknames.

The new crowd was way more fun than the plain kids in Lebanon County. Now Saturday night, which I used to think of as just the night before Sunday, was key to the Rumspringa equation for me and the other Souvenirs. Saturdays were for partying. Wintertime, we'd all get together in a shop or in a barn where there was heat. Summertime, we had our parties in pastures, meadows and open fields. It was always great having parties outside. A lot of kids, boys and girls, were trying cigarettes. So outside was a lot less smoky. We had alcohol too, lots of alcohol. Someone would make a punch and pour different kinds of booze in there. Sometimes, we had bands playing late into the night. That might not seem like a big deal, but except for maybe a harmonica that can be stashed away in a pocket, most Amish people don't play instruments at home or at church. A lot of bishops see playing music as a form of self-expression, and they don't mean that as a compliment. You won't ever hear an organ at Amish Sunday service. Amish sing a lot of hymns, but usually without so much as a pump organ playing along.

So to us, having a band play seemed exciting and slightly taboo. Of course, that made me want to start a band immediately. Lancaster Souvenir parties were filled with people dancing and carrying on. The girls were way friendlier and way more fun than any I'd met in Lebanon. Some of them would actually talk to boys, even someone like seventeen-year-old me, who could be loud and rowdy around his guy friends and suddenly tongue-tied in the presence of a girl.

Lebanon was a long buggy ride from Lancaster on a late Saturday night. I spent a lot of time with my friends' families or staying at one of my sisters' houses. But parents have special radar, and the distance gave me only so much insulation. My parents had heard about these wilder youth groups, and now they were keeping a particular eye on me. My father kept asking me, "How was youth group? What did you do with your friends?" I always gave the vaguest answers possible.

"Not much. Just talked. Hung around."

"Did you enjoy yourself?" he asked.

"Yes, sir," I said, without offering any further details.

Somehow, my mother knew I was drinking. I couldn't figure out how she knew. Maybe the other mothers were gossiping at church on Sunday. Or maybe it was something sneakier than that.

"Were you drinking over the weekend?" she asked more than once.

"No," I insisted.

"I know you were."

"Okay, whatever."

We'd been through this ritual several times already.

One Sunday morning when I was still half-asleep, I heard my mother walk upstairs and into my bedroom. I know it wasn't Monday because my head hurt from drinking so much. There aren't a lot of rules that kids follow about getting drunk, but one I always tried to follow was, "Do your big drinking on Saturday night." Plenty of Amish kids wake up Sunday mornings and say, "Damn, I'll never drink again—or at least not today!" That morning, before my mother told me it was time to wake up, she bent down and put her nose an inch from my mouth. I didn't know what she was doing. I held my eyes closed tight and tried not to breathe. She stayed like that another moment until I had to exhale. Then she stood up, and I heard her satisfied sigh. She'd been smelling my breath all along.

Ah, I thought. *So that's how she knew I'd been drinking!*

My father had his own, quiet way of addressing the subject of alcohol. One Sunday, I stopped at the house with a friend. While we went inside the house to change clothes, I forgot I'd left four six-packs of Yuengling beer in the buggy. And I didn't think to shut the buggy's back end.

My father saw the beer. He didn't say anything. He just went over to the buggy and took the six-packs. When my friend and I got outside, I noticed the back of the buggy was open and the beer was gone.

I said nothing, and neither did my father.

A few months later, I found the empty cans between two rows of corn in the field, where he'd dumped them out. At least I think he dumped them out. He didn't drink the beer, I'm sure of that. Another possibility is that he fed the beer to the cows. Beer is good for sick cows.

I always understood that my parents didn't want me to drink. I also understood that, at this time in my life, they were willing to give me the space to—mostly—figure these things out for myself. I remain grateful to my mom and dad for that. And to this day, I still don't drink around my parents.

My Rumspringa friends and I, we didn't always stay close to home. We went for long drives to places none of us had ever been before, exploring towns in Pennsylvania and into Ohio. We had a whole fleet of cars, from old beat-up junkers that English teenagers would never be caught in to faster, flashier, newer models that somehow we ended up with. It didn't matter to me, as long as it had tires instead of hooves. We hardly bothered with horse-and-buggies at all.

We did all kinds of other stuff, too. Stuff that anyone who wasn't Amish would have considered mundane. We played sports competitively. For the first time in our young lives, we had leagues for softball and flag football and played against teams from other youth groups. We didn't have all the protective equipment that it takes to play tackle, but we sure loved flag football.

I always needed money, even though I'd constantly taken on small pickup work since I was a child. I never felt like I had enough money. Some parents gave their kids spending money, but Dad didn't believe in financing my Rumspringa fun. His idea was: "You don't need money. You're not spending it on the weekend. Your family gets the money. That's how it is." But I did need money, more than an Amish farmer with animals to feed and a family to raise could ever imagine. Now that I was getting out more, I had lots of things to buy. Fast food at the restaurants we hung out in. Little things at the mall that couldn't be called essentials but were still nice to have. I started eyeing some jeans and T-shirts and cool pairs of sneakers. I told myself, "I might not want to dress Amish all the time."

All this meant I'd have to find some steadier part-time jobs, helping out in construction, building things for the neighbors near our house. But again, my father wasn't letting me run completely wild. A lot of other kids in my youth group who had jobs got to keep the money they earned. But from my part-time jobs, my father always expected me to give him the checks—the whole checks. He might give me back 10 percent, but that didn't leave much in my pocket. I was supposed to keep turning the checks over until I was twenty-one. At that rate, I knew I'd have to work an awful lot of part-time jobs or lots of full-time jobs just to make enough money to pay for all the new exciting things I was experiencing. So I found little ways to keep some of my money. When I got paid, I did give my father the checks. But every time I finished a job, I'd keep the last check for myself. Dad never thought to keep track of my start and end dates.

Whether I was at home in Lebanon or in Lancaster with my uncles, I still went with my family to church most of the time unless I'd been out really late on Saturday night. But just because it was church day didn't mean Rumspringa came to a grinding halt. Sunday afternoons, we played volleyball and drank some more. We still had singing. Every group, no matter how plain or adventurous they were, had to sing Christian hymns on Sunday night. But the Souvenirs didn't see that as a chore. My new friends actually seemed to like singing together. This whole crowd was much more to my liking, and I think they liked me, too. I wasn't the only one who had a haircut anymore.

It probably wasn't so different from the stuff normal teenagers anywhere in America were doing, including underage drinking. But we weren't normal teenagers. We understood that. We were Amish. These experiences were different enough from the way we were raised, they seemed daring.

As different as these new experiences were to me, there is one other thing that stands out in my mind. The same way I felt close to my older brothers, I started to feel close with some of the guys in my group. A lot of the time, my new friends and I just hung out. Then we started talking. Tentatively at first, we expressed our feelings and frustrations about our lives. A lot of us agreed about how tough we had it growing up. We'd all had some of the same experiences. We were at the same age and in the same place in life—finished school at eighth grade, trying to figure out what was coming next for us, often without any clue at all. We *got* each other. That's all. I learned I wasn't the only one who sometimes felt confused about exactly where I fit in this unusual world of ours and what it really meant to be Amish.

CHAPTER 5
OPEN ROAD

Rumspringa was never supposed to be what it eventually became, a big, rule-breaking blowout for the young and Amish.

There's a common misconception that Amish parents encourage, even want, their children to go totally wild during Rumspringa and explore hidden alleys the church doesn't approve of. Nothing could be farther from the truth. The original idea was that teenage boys and girls needed a time when they'd be allowed to ease up on chores so they could date, find a spouse and prepare for adulthood. But over many years, Amish kids did what kids always do. They were given an inch, and they took seventeen miles.

I bought my first car when I was eighteen. Without even realizing it, my father helped me pay for that car. A few years earlier, he had given me a little Angus bull calf he had in the barn. He told me I could keep the calf as a pet and then sell it when I was ready. That turned out to be a tactical error on my father's part. I raised the calf, and then I sold it for $900. I took $500 of the money and bought a light-brown 1986 Pontiac Grand Prix. I found the car in the *Merchandiser* newspaper, which was filled with little classified ads—

Craigslist before there was Craigslist. The car was long and low and wide as a boat. No one would have called that car pretty, but growing up like I did, going everywhere by horse-and-buggy, I could hardly believe I had my own set of wheels—the rubber, inflatable kind.

I already had my license. I had convinced my brother Sam to take me to the driver's license office. Many of my new Rumspringa friends already had driver's licenses. I wanted one, too. The problem was that being a minor, I needed my parents to sign for me, and I wouldn't dare ask them. Sam agreed to sign as my guardian. I walked out with a learner's permit.

I'd been driving tractors since I was a little kid. I'd driven buggies for years. But I didn't have much experience behind the wheel of an actual automobile. The first time I drove alone, I was craving ice cream. I borrowed my stepbrother Daniel's VW Rabbit and drove to the neighbor's house where we kept our freezer, one foot on the accelerator, one foot on the brake, choppy all the way.

By the time I bought the Grand Prix with the bull-calf money, I didn't even have to hide the car from my father anymore. My older brothers had paved the way for me. The first time an Amish truck pulled into our driveway to pick up one of them, my dad grabbed a shotgun and marched out front. "I'm gonna blow your tires out if you don't get that thing off this property!" he barked.

Eventually, my brothers just wore my father down. When my brothers got their own first cars, he didn't like it. But he didn't go nuts. They parked out in the field or behind one of the neighbors' houses. There was a clearing back there, and it made a fine parking lot. My dad knew what they were doing, but as long as the neighbors didn't think he was explicitly condoning it, he didn't make a fuss. And eventually, even that distinction faded away. A few years later when my stepbrothers got cars, my dad still didn't like it, but he really never brought the issue up. When I showed up with a car, he'd either given up or he just didn't care anymore. I parked the Grand Prix out behind the barn—on the property, just not where every passing bishop would see.

I still wore Amish clothes to leave the house, but I changed as soon as I got into the car. I pulled my plain black pants off and had jeans underneath. In the summer, it was shorts and a T-shirt. I think my parents knew I was doing this, but I was trying to show some respect to them. I guess they gave me the respect of not bugging me in return. I did that for a while, but even that charade finally ended. My parents seemed happy to look the other way, and I breathed another sigh of relief. I definitely had things easier than my brothers did.

That car was good for my social life. I was also growing more confident with this new environment called the outside world. Now I could stay out later, make longer trips, connect with more people and find better parties and bars. I'm not saying these were the most important things in the world, but they were an important part of experiencing life, which I hadn't done a lot of. We had some great parties in those days. None were better than what we called band hops, which happened a couple of times a year. Those events were legendary, like Woodstock or Coachella for the Amish. People would talk about them for weeks. We'd set up in an open field or at someone's house when their parents were away. We'd roll in a large, wooden wagon and use that as a stage for bands to play on. Amish kids don't have to rent from the local party-supply center, we always knew how to build stuff. We built stages, bars, dance floors, every-thing. If we couldn't find electric lines to connect to, we'd bring in generators.

There was alcohol, of course. And drugs, too. I can't deny it. Cocaine and marijuana mostly. I've heard people mention even harder stuff, but I never saw any of that at our parties—maybe they had it at other peoples' parties, I don't know. I heard a girl my age overdosed in Ohio. That may or may not be true. Our parties were all about lots of young people who needed to have a great time. Big crowds turned out—two hundred, three hundred, five hundred people on a Saturday night. Male and female, people from near and far, every age of unmarried Amish from sixteen to about thirty years old.

Even though we were doing these things in plain sight, we didn't really want the elders paying close attention. But the preachers occasionally caught word that a band hop was happening, and you knew they just wouldn't turn a blind eye. If your preacher found out you'd gone to one of these parties, you had to go to church and confess and ask forgiveness. That's how famous these parties became. There were actual guidelines that the preachers and bishops all seemed to follow.

No one wanted to get caught, but those who did dutifully put on their Amish clothes and confessed. Not because they were afraid of eternal damnation. If that were the case, no Amish kid would dare go near those band hops. They did it to make themselves look better in the eyes of the community. It would be embarrassing for their parents if they simply ignored the church elders. So they promised to do better, and the church members were pleased that "Ephram and Leah realized they were wrong." Then, just as predictably, the freshly chastised partiers would start asking when the next band hop would be.

I know we didn't invent any of this. Teenagers have been having large, unsupervised parties for generations, probably as long as there have been teenagers. But the fact that we were Amish and we were doing it, too—that was mammoth. Amish and non-Amish both found it hard to believe, and I didn't see any reason to stop.

When I was twenty-one, I started playing in a rock band. No, it wasn't officially allowed. But yes, some Amish people do play in bands. My uncles John and David both played guitar. I'd been seeing a lot of bands, but they were the ones who got me interested. They used to play some pretty big parties for their time. They had some great stories to tell. The story I loved hearing most was about a night they played in a very large barn. Everyone was dancing and having a wonderful time, but the crowd was so large that right in the middle of a fast song, the barn floor collapsed. Incredibly, perhaps miraculously, no one was hurt. The Amish are not quitters, and they were certainly enjoying themselves, so the dancers just stepped away from the hole in the floor and kept moving to the beat.

"They were too far gone to make them stop," Uncle David would say.

I remember thinking: "Music, sweat, dancing, being in such a frenzy that I wouldn't even notice if the floor caved in—that's something I can see myself in the middle of." But except for some barrels, pots and pans that could stand in for a drum set, I didn't have a musical instrument to play.

It's an Amish tradition that when a boy turns sixteen his father gets a horse-and-buggy for him. That way, he'll be able to get around on the weekends. For a while I liked not having to ask my parents or older brothers for rides. But the truth was that I was never too interested in horse-and-buggies, not even the fancier ones some kids fixed up. After I got my car, I completely quit using the horse my dad got for me. So I sold it for $1,200 and used the money to buy a Fender amplifier and a Gibson bass guitar.

The band we started was called the Nighthawks. There were five of us. We played mostly eighties rock—Bob Seger, Tom Petty, John Mellencamp, some Rolling Stones—and we played some country. None of us was a great musician. But we were loud. And there is nothing like the thrill of being onstage while everyone in the room is getting into the music. It didn't take long for me to understand why my uncles loved recounting every minute of their stage experience. It wasn't too Amish, but it was an awful lot of fun. I'd been fitting a lot of new things into my life in the years since I'd found my way to the right youth group. Playing in a band was just one more experience that opened my eyes.

As I got older, the more I kept seeking new experiences. More and more, my friends and I were hanging out in bars.

For one thing, most of us were finally legal, although the drinking laws weren't enforced nearly as strictly as they are today. For another, nearly everyone I knew was getting a car, and it was far easier to get around. Those horse-and-buggies kind of stick out in a tavern parking lot, not to mention they look very uncool.

Usually, we wore English clothes. I really didn't like going into a bar dressed Amish. I thought it was disrespectful. At least I would take off my suspenders, my hat and my coat. I knew how the English talked when they saw an Amish person come into a bar. You could hear the whispers immediately.

"What's he doing in here?"

"Is he supposed to be in here?"

"I'm gonna call his bishop."

"Hey, Yam!" That's an old slur for Amish. "Wanna dance?"

I just shrugged and smiled. Sometimes, I sent over a round of drinks. I liked being in new environments, but I wasn't looking for trouble unless trouble was looking for me.

Soon enough, my friends and I found some places that became our own. We liked Shooter's Crossing in New Holland and YP, which stood for Your Place and was right off Route 30. But Doughboy's became our favorite. It was easy for our friends to find, a rustic wooden building with a high-pitched red roof and a green door off Route 23 in Leola. We knew the bartenders and a lot of the people in there, and the place was always hopping. It filled up on weekends with a combination of regulars and new faces. They served drinks and pizza and had a pool table in the back. I was pretty good at eight ball. There was always sports on the TVs. We'd watch baseball or basketball, but when fall rolled around, football was really our game. Most of my friends were Eagles fans. Some liked the Steelers, but Lancaster County was basically Eagles country. Maybe once a year, a bunch of us would even drive to Veterans Stadium in Philadelphia. That was huge for us. Around that time, the Eagles' fans completely hated the Dallas Cowboys. We yelled ourselves hoarse trash-talking "America's Team." I would not have wanted to be a Cowboys fan who wandered into Doughboy's.

A lot of guys had a sidekick, a best friend who'd tag along for the night. Quacky was mine. Or maybe he'd say I was his. Wherever one of us was, the other one wasn't far away. His real name was David, but he got the nickname before I ever met him, when he was fifteen or sixteen. He was quacking like a duck or something, I don't know. Whatever it was, he'd outgrown it. Quacky lived about fifteen minutes from my house so we took turns driving. He's married now, but back then he was a lot like I was. He was a little crazy and knew how to have fun anywhere. He didn't care where we went or what we did. And did I mention his father was a preacher?

They always say in the Amish community, "The clergy's kids are the worst." I saw that a lot. The stricter your parents were, the crazier you turned out to be. Quacky and I had that in common, his father being a preacher, mine being a deacon. We definitely had similar personalities, not caring too much what other people thought.

We were often inseparable, but if we were lucky some girls would also come out with us. A lot of times that changed our regular plans and calmed us down. Sometimes, if the girls would come along, we'd go bowling or play miniature golf or some other stupid stuff like that, just to be able to hang out with them. Amish girls weren't as wild as the boys. They would drink some, though not as much as we or the English girls did—or the English boys for that matter. Most of the time, the girls wouldn't even sit up at the bar. They would come inside and get a table and order a slice. They'd have water. Some of the girls would get looser on weekends and drink on Saturday nights, but not very many. And I wouldn't call it dating, what we did, not the way English teenagers did. Not even close. Mostly, it was Quacky and me and maybe a couple of other guy friends and, if we were lucky, a couple of girls. We'd all hang out together. Then we'd all head home.

Sex? Yes, of course—*in my dreams!* Our parents might have thought we were flying out of control, but we were easing into the outside world very, very slowly. We were still Amish. Our female friends were always Amish. The farthest I ever got with any of them was the most fleeting fooling around.

Looking back on those days, there are a few things I do regret. Probably the biggest one: We did a lot of driving way too drunk to do it safely. It really is a miracle we didn't kill someone. Some higher power must have been listening to my mother's prayers.

Some nights, I would drive between Lancaster and Lebanon and not even know how I'd gotten home. I'm not proud of that at all. I never hurt anyone or myself, but I didn't completely get away with it, either.

One night we were at Doughboy's, and a guy wanted a ride home to Lancaster. I didn't know him. But he asked, and I said, "Sure." I gave him the ride. I don't even remember how far it was or how long it took. Then I went back to the bar to catch up with my friends. But when I got inside, the bartender told me that they'd already moved on to a diner on Route 23. I went back out to the parking lot and got into my car. Just as I pulled out of Doughboy's, a cop threw his lights and siren on. I didn't come close to passing the sobriety test.

My second drunk-driving arrest, there wasn't a bar in sight, but there was no shortage of alcohol. It was after a camping trip. We'd been up all night drinking. I remember I got only about two hours' sleep. Those Lancaster County sheriff's deputies seemed to be everywhere. Again, I was pulled over and again, I flunked the test. This time, though, they didn't just ticket and fine me. Since it was my second offense, I served twenty-eight days in jail.

There's so much talk about the wild and crazy things Amish kids do when they taste a little freedom. Some of that talk is true. But the vast majority of what we did in my Rumspringa days, I look back on with pride and pleasure.

It revealed a world I hardly knew existed. I learned some things about myself I had never even thought about. I gained some confidence and some understanding, though all of it came at a price. My faith would never be as unquestioning again.

CHAPTER 6
COURTING TROUBLE

"Go talk to her," the girl's friend said to me. "She likes you. You should talk to her."

So I worked up my courage. I traded glances with Quacky and my other friends. I walked over and spoke to the girl, who had blue eyes, angular features and a long, perfect nose. Her name was Sarah. Of course it was. Every third Amish girl, it seems, is Sarah.

"Hi," I said.

No response.

"Hi," I said again. "How you doin'?"

"Fine."

It was the stingiest, tiniest, most reluctant *fine* imaginable. It definitely didn't say, "Hi, thanks for coming over. I've been hoping you'd come talk to me." This *fine* was more like, "What made you decide to bother me?" The *fine* was followed by a blank, bored stare.

Amish girls are hard to talk to and harder to date. They have ways of repelling guys they're not interested in and ways of getting the ones they want. They'll check you out. They'll move on quickly. If you're not their type, whatever that is, they won't give you five minutes of their time. Maybe later, when everyone grows older, the guys might be the ones running the businesses and making decisions on the farm. But when young people are at the age of pairing off, those meek-looking, fresh-faced girls are totally in charge.

It is the girl who starts the relationship. It's the girl who breaks it off. It isn't what the guy wants that matters. It's what the girl wants. Targeting prospects, narrowing the field, making selections, planning dates, going steady, getting baptized, getting hitched—the boys are there, they're included, but they're mostly along for the ride.

"Okay," I said with a shrug to one-word Sarah before I walked away.

These girls have their own reconnaissance system and advance teams. Their friends will summon you to get a better look. They will lure you in with encouraging talk: "You should date her." When you get to the point of finally asking her out, the girl will just as likely cut you off. Those shy, reclusive Amish girls have a very clear idea of who they want to be with. They don't believe in settling. They are certain they will get that guy.

It wasn't just me. Back in those awkward days, many of my male friends got the same treatment. I've gotten a little better at this stuff over the years. I've built up my confidence. I've become more comfortable talking with girls, which isn't saying too much, I know, because I started out so clumsy. But even now, I'd say, the girls and the women are firmly in charge of the social side of living Amish. They have things right about where they want them. They like things the old-fashioned way.

Let's face facts: Most single Amish people won't be finding their soul mates on Match.com—or even ChristianMingle or eHar-

mony. First, there's the issue of Internet access without electricity. Then there's the culture of bashfulness, the stern prohibition
on dating outside the faith and the stylistic challenges of white
bonnets and black hats. There are other practical hurdles as well:
Not too many English singles want to go courting by horse-and-
buggy.

Yes, being Amish does present some special dating challenges.

In fact, most of today's other popular venues for pairing off aren't
available to the Amish. We don't go to coed high schools. Heck, we
don't go to *any* high schools. There's no college or grad school, much
less fraternity mixers and boy-girl dorms. Our early jobs usually
don't present many dating prospects, either. Who are we going to
meet on the family farm? Our older siblings? The occasional visiting
cousin? A few of our precocious friends might have found lifelong
sweethearts in seventh grade, but that's no easy trick when the one-
room Amish school has a total enrollment of thirty or thirty-five students, and you're already related to half of them. But for most of us,
that leaves the traditional Amish hunting grounds—church, family
setups, youth groups, and the weddings of relatives and friends. For
the marriage-minded Amish, the old ways are the best ways all over
again. And the stakes couldn't be higher. Short of deciding between
heaven and hell, choosing a mate is the most important decision
an Amish person will ever be invited to make. Divorce, after all, is
strictly forbidden.

Given all we're up against, it's amazing anyone ever pairs off.

Somehow or another, young Amish adults need to find lifelong
partners who share their values, customs and outlook—and, ide-
ally, who are smoking hot. Okay, that last one isn't mentioned in the
Ordnung. But I've known a lot of young Amish men and women

in their prime marriage-eligible years. Just like people everywhere, they want someone they are excited about, even if the Amish criteria for smoking hot might seem a little odd. There's no going for the girl who dresses sexiest in a modest calf-length dress. These girls don't wear makeup because they're not supposed to draw attention to themselves. Still, the Amish have their own romance checklists. Everybody does. Strong back? Check. Sturdy thighs? Check. Appears fertile? Check. Kind heart? Check. Nice smile? Double check.

This all sets off a careful Amish courting ritual.

When a possible connection is made and the guy believes he's finally gotten the nod to proceed, he might offer the girl a ride home in his buggy, then go inside to meet her parents. If all goes well, the young couple will sit in the parlor and talk awhile. If Mom likes the pairing, she may bring out a plate of homemade cookies or some cheese straws. And if things keep clicking, the guy and girl could eventually decide to go steady.

Going steady doesn't mean they'll be together constantly—more like once a week. Every other Sunday, they can see each other at church, then hang around after the service to talk and sing with the other young people. It's the non-church weekends when there's time for a Saturday-night date, just the two of them. They don't even need to drag the Rumspringa posse along. Will it be hot chocolate in the back of the buggy? Or reciting favorite Bible verses together from memory? Or sharing dreams of many children and a many-acred farm? Or will the evening be filled with racier intentions? Will the young couple sneak out to their secret spot behind the barn? When you're young and Amish and possibly in love, you know that someone's always watching—and those prying eyes can be human or divine. It all comes down to what your own beliefs are and how much risk you want to take.

Many Amish teenagers have premarital sex, just like teens in other places do. Are they having more sex or less sex? We could debate that all day. The truth is there are no reliable surveys on Amish kids doing it. And don't hold your breath. Because we aren't likely to get good data on this any time soon. Amish sixteen-year-olds probably won't report their next grope-and-grind session to Gallup or Quinnipiac any more than they'll report it to their parents or to the bishop. And you probably won't find good evidence on Facebook, either. There's the occasional Amish-teen status update from a forbidden smartphone, but Amish teens tend to use sites like Facebook, Instagram and Twitter with extra discretion and modesty, when they use social media at all. All I'm saying is, please, don't believe all the chastity talk. Amish parents are mostly kidding themselves when they say, "Oh, our fine youngsters wouldn't dare be involved in anything like sex! They're too busy canning vegetables and singing hymns!"

As if!

Here's what I know from my own experiences and those of many friends, relatives, neighbors and bar-stool companions: The Amish may live on farms in out-of-the-way places, but we aren't stuck in flyover country as far as youthful hormones are concerned. God may be standing guard over all of us, but anatomy and biology haven't thrown in the towel yet.

From holding hands to making out to reaching down to—well, you get my point. The only thing I will say for certain is this: In my group, the early attempts were clumsy, wrapped up in awkwardness, inexperience and guilt. And we all thought about sex a whole lot more than we were doing it.

But except for the suspenders and prim bonnets, didn't that make us about the same as young people everywhere?

Not long ago, I asked some of my Amish friends how much sex education they got at home. The answers came in about like I expected:

"Not a word."

"The night before I got married, my father sat me down. He seemed very uncomfortable. 'Um, if there's anything you want to know about, just ask me, okay?' I said there wasn't. He said, 'Good.'"

"The only sex education I got," one female friend said, "was watching a litter of kittens be born at our neighbor's house. My mother wasn't happy when she heard I'd seen that. I thought I might be going to hell. But actually, that taught me a lot about where babies come from. Farm kids don't stay in the dark too long."

My father did what he could to keep us there. He never had a birds-and-bees talk with me or any of my brothers. He even made sure I wasn't in the barn when he was arranging for the cows and bulls to breed. God knows how that might have scarred me!

Several of my female friends said their mothers had warned them about getting their periods—or at least comforted them afterward by explaining that they weren't dying. But most of my friends, male and female, said they picked up a lot of what they learned in little snatches from friends, cousins and older siblings. Some of that information was probably exaggerated or just plain wrong. (*"I'm not sure, but I think you might get pregnant from French-kissing a boy!"*) And frankly, being on the back side of the sex-education curve, I'm not sure our knowledge was ever all that complete. Even today, I sometimes joke about my own lingering cluelessness: "You'd really be amazed at how much I still don't know!"

I'll bet you already know the traditional Amish view on sex. It can be summed up in exactly four words: "Go forth and multiply." Genesis 1:22 stretches it out to nine: "And God blessed them, saying, 'Be fruitful, and multiply.'" And then you have one more important wrinkle: All that is supposed to happen *after getting married*. Marriage, sex, babies—in that order and, hopefully, without any unnecessary delay. Ever since Jakob Ammann roamed the earth, his followers and descendants have been told over and over again in no uncertain terms: Sex isn't for fun. It's for making babies. Now, get busy, kids!

The Amish have certainly taken that message to heart, continuing to see children as a precious gift from God. It would be rude, wouldn't it, to refuse God's gift—or six or eight or ten of them? There's a practical side to this, as well: the old farm-family view of children as extra hands at planting and harvest time. Those aren't just hungry mouths to feed! Those are little farm workers who will soon be ready to sweep the barn or help out in the fields!

The numbers don't lie: Six or seven children—that's normal for Amish families. It's also two or three times the size of a typical American Catholic family, a group that once had a reputation for producing large broods. I know our own blended Stoltzfus-Peachey clan helped pull the average up a little. But our fifteen didn't raise any eyebrows in Lebanon County, I promise you that. And we were total amateurs compared to the Troyers of Kokomo,

Indiana. John Troyer was married to Catherine Schrock. Together, they had twelve children. That's a good-sized family but far from shocking by Amish standards. Then Catherine died and John married her cousin, Caroline Schrock Kendall, a young widow with two children. Then John and Caroline had seventeen children together for a total of thirty-one. No one can know for sure if that's an Amish record, but there are twenty-nine Troyers who can say today, "I'm a middle child."

I'll admit, that's a little extreme. But every Amish person knows a family or two like the Troyers. And the average Amish family isn't likely to shrink much in the years to come. The Amish elders still stand where they always have on the question of birth control, and that birth-control rule can be summed up in two words: "Hell no!" They forbid anything that gets in the way of more children, especially a condom, a diaphragm or a birth-control pill. They don't even condone so-called natural family-planning techniques like the rhythm method. In recent years, there's been a very slight thawing on this, emphasis on very slight. No church leaders have announced any policy changes, and very few Amish couples will admit in public to using birth control. A few will quietly tell you they do for "medical reasons" or "because the doctor told [them] to."

But for now, "Amish family" and "large Amish family" mean almost exactly the same thing. And it almost always starts with a large Amish wedding.

By tradition, all these moves are laid out in intricate detail. It's like all Amish lives and futures are written in a dusty old book somewhere, and we get handed the pages one at a time.

Most Amish weddings are held in November or December, which makes sense because that's when the harvest is over and the heavy farm work is done. There's nothing the Amish are better at than sensible tradition. Even in families that don't live on farms, it's almost unheard of to plan a big June wedding. Who would be able to come at the height of the growing and tourist season? Late fall is wedding time, and Tuesdays and Thursdays are the favorite days, giving the bride's family extra time to prepare before and clean up after without bumping into Sunday services. That brief two-month window doesn't leave many open days to choose from. During "wedding season," many Amish people are invited to two or three weddings per week.

All Amish weddings are like all other Amish weddings. I've never had a wedding myself. But believe me, I've attended enough of them to know the script line by line.

The bride usually makes her own wedding dress out of blue or purple fabric. Her two attendants make dresses from the same material. All three women will wear Amish prayer capes and aprons. Like everything else Amish, nothing goes to waste. After she's married, the bride will wear that dress to church on Sundays. And when death does them part, she'll wear that dress to be buried in. The Amish groom and his two attendants will wear black suits, white shirts, black-brimmed hats, black high-topped boots and, in a break from every other day, when no neckwear is allowed, black bow ties. There are no wedding rings, no flowers and no veils.

Amish weddings are considered hugely festive occasions. Nothing for the Amish is more joyous than seeing two of their own joined in wedlock. It's the culmination of every parent's dream from the time the children are born. Before the wedding, both the bride and groom will join the church and be baptized. That alone is cause for a sigh of parental relief. A marriage is a promise to continue the faith, and everyone hopes that the happy couple will soon be starting their own very large Amish family together. Those things all call for major celebration.

People often ask me if the Amish have arranged marriages. I laugh and say, "I hope someone arranges a good one for me." The truth is, Amish parents don't actually choose who their children marry, but they do have a voice. A minister won't agree to preside over the ceremony if all four parents don't approve of the union. And the Amish aren't above a little pre-wedding mediating. My father tells me that as a deacon, he often has to smooth the way before a wedding can take place. The boy's family thinks the girl's family isn't devout enough. The girl's family worries the boy won't be stern enough to raise righteous children. It could be anything.

The plans are kept quiet until two weeks before the big day. No sparkling rocks on the bride-to-be's third finger. No save-the-date cards. No pre-engagement parties. Only then, when everyone's agreed and both families have given their blessing, are the couple's plans "published" and the congregation is officially informed. But even before that, it's hard to keep things totally secret. Some little signs can hint beforehand that a wedding might be in the works. Watch for the celery. As soon as a girl tells her parents she is planning to marry, they will plant an extra patch of celery near the house. Celery is considered lucky for an Amish couple. Lots of it will be served on the wedding day. So a sighting of feathery celery leaves can always get the local women buzzing.

You won't find Amish parents touring local wedding halls. And the young couple won't be planning an island destination wedding.

How would they even get there? Most weddings are held at the bride's family's home. But with such large families, the guest lists are rarely short. Two hundred to three hundred of their closest friends and relatives will likely attend, as many as the house can hold and then some. Those who come from far away will hire a van and driver. No church member wants to be seen driving a car up to an Amish wedding.

The day starts with a long church service held right there at home, complete with many hymns and a long sermon. The Amish are used to that. The wedding ceremony, which is fairly simple, follows immediately. The ceremony begins with the minister counseling the bride and groom, making sure they understand that Amish marriage is permanent. The couple is then asked to make their vows. As you might expect, the Amish aren't too big on writing their own.

I wouldn't call the vows especially romantic. The minister's questions are designed more to have the couple restate their religious faith, with a little caring thrown in. "Can you both confess and believe that God has ordained marriage to be a union between one man and one wife, and do you also have the confidence that you are approaching marriage in accordance with the way you have been taught?"

And "Do you also have confidence, brother, that the Lord has provided this, our sister, as a marriage partner for you?" And "Do you promise your husband that if he should in bodily weakness, sickness or any similar circumstances need your help, that you will care for him as is fitting for a Christian wife?" And "Will you with love, forbearance and patience live with each other and not part from each other until God will separate you by death?"

Once the bride and groom have agreed to all that, the union is blessed, and a final prayer is said.

The bride and groom do not kiss. The minister doesn't pronounce them "Mr. and Mrs." But with the minister's hand covering the bride and groom's clasped hands, they are married.

Then it's party time.

The jubilation begins immediately with a large, noontime, celery-accented meal: cut-celery appetizer, roasted chicken (my mother calls it hingleflesh) with celery stuffing, creamed celery as the main vegetable, grumbatta mush (that's mashed potatoes) and gravy, salads, cheese, bologna, bread, butter, honey, jelly, fruits, pies, pudding, ice cream and little centerpiece jars with celery stalks on every table. The tables are arranged around the edge of the living room and throughout the first floor of the house, wherever there is wall space. A special table, called an Eck, is set up in the corner for the bridal party. The bride takes the traditional seat to the left of her groom, symbolizing where she will sit in their marriage buggy. The single Amish women sit on the bride's side of the room. The single Amish men sit on the groom's side. The couples' parents and siblings sit together in the kitchen. Why they do that, I don't know.

After everyone's finished eating, the wedding cakes—plural—are brought out. Some are made by the neighbor women who pitched in to help prepare the feast. But there's usually one from a local bakery, saved for later in the day.

This is truly a big day for everyone. So even after the long ceremony and huge servings of food, the Amish wedding rituals have barely begun. Amish nuptials have an added secret agenda. Single young men and women know that late fall isn't just wedding season. It's also meet-your-mate time. Many of the activities are designed to pair off the bride's and groom's single friends, a key responsibility of every newlywed couple. An especially large fuss is always made over "going to the table." After the noon meal is over, the unmarried women ages sixteen to thirty are invited to sit in one of the upstairs bedrooms. The men walk out to the barn, where, I know from painful experience, they stand around uncomfortably and joke with one another about what is coming next. Two married couples—friends of the bride and groom—join the young men in the barn and, in a key part of the tradition, convince them to go upstairs. That's where the pairing off will begin. Each guy has to enter the bedroom filled with anxious, giggling girls and ask one of the young ladies to "go to the table." When the new "couple" finally emerges, a roomful of curious eyes follow as they walk down the stairs hand in hand, then sit together at a long wooden table for the next round of food.

This is tradition, and all Amish guys have been through it. That walk down the stairs can be painful if you're shy. More than once, I've wondered if the parents of the girl I'd asked to the table weren't watching me closely, judging my suitability for their daughter. I have no idea how I might have measured up. But mostly, it's good fun for the wedding guests, whether they are involved or not. There's a lot of nervous laughter and sideward glances involved. The hope is that a few boy-girl connections will be made and romantic sparks will fly. The older folks watch all this knowingly from chairs and benches around the house, often breaking into song with rousing hymns. The singing continues for hours while more food is served and young people get better acquainted.

At some point in the evening, the unmarried women are invited out to the barn to mingle with the unmarried men. This can be especially entertaining if any fresh boy-girl connections have been made.

It can also be torture. At weddings of friends, I've experienced both. The bride and groom try to make sure that all the unmarried men and women have partners for the evening, even if some of the pairings don't click perfectly.

As the evening rolls on, everyone wanders back to the house. The heat is up. The gaslights are glowing. Some of the men might take a nip or two of homemade liquor. There is another meal, more talking, and the hymnals come out again. Finally, sometime around ten or eleven o'clock, everyone shuffles out to the buggies and vans for the groggy ride home.

Amish newlyweds might not get right down to the business of starting a family on the wedding night. They usually spend their honeymoon weekend at the girl's parents' home. The new husband stops shaving immediately. That beard will become his Amish wedding ring. Then the happy couple spend the next few months traveling each weekend to the homes of different relatives, being fed and feted and collecting furniture, quilts and other wedding gifts. Only then are the young newlyweds ready to move into a home of their own. By then, the husband's beard should have grown out a little, letting everyone see immediately that he is a married man.

So does this whole system work? Does it bring together suitable Amish couples who love each other, stay together and go forth and multiply like they are supposed to? The numbers say yes, absolutely. The divorce rate is down near zero. Family size vacillates between giant and huge. And the vast majority of married Amish couples stay together the rest of their lives. Some of this "commitment" is surely because of the powerful social pressure the Amish live with every day. Those who get divorced are usually forced to leave the church as well. So their busted unions often don't get counted as failed Amish marriages. Statistics aren't supposed to lie, but they don't always tell the whole truth, either.

It's hard to prove for certain one way or the other. My own personal impressions tell me . . . mostly, yes. Most Amish marriages achieve what they are supposed to.

And it really does make sense. From what I've seen, most Amish people seem to get along fairly well with the people they've married, probably as well as people in any other faith. Maybe a little better, in fact. The Amish start their marriages with a big advantage over many other couples. For the most part, they've all been raised alike with expectations and experiences that are extraordinarily similar. What does the newly married couple have in common? Almost everything!

There are other things to take into consideration when trying to explain the staying power of Amish couples. As a group, the Amish aren't big complainers. When they suffer, they tend to suffer in silence. They're told to take their burdens and offer them up to the Lord.

Other religions worry constantly about empty churches, shrinking families, intermarriage and loss of faith. Those aren't really problems in the Amish community, and the rituals of Amish mating serve to reinforce all that.

I've given a lot of thought to this in my own life: If I had found an Amish girlfriend and gotten married to her, maybe I would have stayed Old Order Amish. Maybe I would have gotten baptized in the Amish church. Maybe I would have had ten or fifteen children. Maybe I would have led a very different life.

Maybe, maybe, maybe.

As things turned out, that path wasn't my path. I was born into the Amish community. I stayed very much in the Amish community. But I continue to find my own route through life.

I'm not sure if that makes me a success or a failure, but it definitely makes me who I am.

CHAPTER 7
SO ORDERED

"**Y**ou should ask that one out," my mother told me.

She was talking about an Amish girl, the daughter of a friend of hers, who was—let me be frank here—just about the last girl on earth I would choose to date.

Then my mother focused on another girl, who made the first one look like Kelly McGillis in *Witness*. "She's very nice," my mother insisted. "That's the one you should take out. You'll like her—definitely."

"I don't think so," I told my mother.

"You should do it."

"You can't just go over and ask them out," I said, reaching for excuses. "It has to be someone you already know."

"Just do it," my mother said.

"You don't understand."

It wasn't just my mother. I know my father felt the same way, though he wasn't quite as vocal with the dating advice. Both my parents wanted me to find an Amish girlfriend—and not because they were concerned about my social life. Thanks to Rumspringa, my social life was going great. My parents wanted me to get an Amish girlfriend, because they believed that might be the only way I would quit dragging my feet about getting baptized in the Old Order Amish Church.

I was in my early twenties. After five or six years of Rumspringa, many of my friends had gotten baptized. Some of them had also married. It was almost always the same scenario: The Amish guy got an Amish girlfriend. The girl wanted to get married. Both of them knew the rules: To get married in the Old Order Amish Church, you had to be baptized in the Old Order Amish Church. With every new baptism and marriage, the Anabaptist faith of Jacob Ammann and others would be handed down to another Amish generation and on and on, as it always had been and probably always will be. And the young couple's lucky parents would be blessed with grandchildren, too.

My mother did not give up easily. I know she and my father were getting pressure from people at church who wondered what was up with "that Levi."

"If you die young," she said to me, test-driving another argument, "it would be best if you were baptized." All of this was sincere, I know. She didn't want her youngest son heading off to hell.

I didn't tell my parents this, but the girls I liked were mostly English. Nothing super serious or long-term had developed yet. I hadn't ruled out Amish girls. I'd have been happy to settle down with one if we connected, but that hadn't happened so far, no matter how many daughters my mother's friends might have had.

As far as I was concerned, there were arguments on both sides.

I believed in God. There was no doubt about that. I was raised Amish and felt Amish. Amish was what I knew. I embraced the core Amish values of love, support and community. But when I was truthful with myself, I also knew I'd been experiencing doubt for a long time that the Old Order Amish Church was the one way to heaven for me. I had some real problems with how things were run.

The rigidity. The contradictions. The hypocrisy. The fixation on hard-to-explain rules. The iron-willed authority of bishops who seemed to be making it up as they went along—and then sometimes disagreed with the bishop up the road. The weird inconsistencies that had been weighing on my mind for years. I couldn't find any of that in the Bible. Should you really shun someone you love just to teach them a lesson? Was it really okay to bully families you thought weren't devout enough? Even Jesus wasn't that judgmental!

Then there was my behavior. For several years already, I'd been doing things that would not be permitted once I joined the church. Driving, drinking, dressing English, playing in a rock band, watching TV, thinking about certain girls in certain ways—so many things I couldn't have listed them all in one of those black-and-white composition books we used to carry to Amish school. I'd been experiencing so many things I found I enjoyed, and none of it was church approved. I knew if I got baptized, I'd be promising to give all those things up.

But here was an interesting wrinkle: No matter what I'd been doing until this point, I hadn't broken a single rule of the Amish church. Not one. The reason for that was simple: Even though I'd been raised in an Amish home by Amish parents, even though I started going to Amish services before I got my first black hat, I hadn't yet been baptized in the Amish church. So I wasn't officially

Amish. I was beholden to my parents. I lived under their authority. They had every right to be mad at me or disappointed in me or worried about me. But I wasn't bound by the Ordnung. None of the church's rules applied to me, yet.

Nice technicality, huh?

Once I got baptized, though, that would all change. From that point forward, I'd also be responsible to the church.

Believer's baptism, free-will baptism, adult baptism—call it what you will. That's what the Anabaptist tradition is all about. Your faith and commitment aren't imposed on you in childhood. You accept them or decline them once you become an adult.

To me, this was serious business. I had friends who'd been living loose and free like I had. They got baptized and married, promising before God and the church and everyone to follow the straight-and-narrow path. Then they broke that promise almost immediately and just kept living like they pleased. It seemed to me it would be better not making promises in the first place, if I didn't plan on keeping them. Baptism, I believed, was a permanent, solemn vow to follow the church and the many rules of the Ordnung. I'm not saying those rules aren't bent and broken by plenty of Amish people. But I knew that if I kept doing the things that I'd been doing in my Rumspringa time, I'd be shattering that vow into a million pieces. I could be punished, shunned or excommunicated, and I'd probably feel awful about myself. There's not a lot of wiggle room after baptism.

"I'm thinking about it," I told my father when he asked me about my intentions. "I just don't know."

• • •

In my crowd, there were some families who were far more rigid than my parents were. They insisted their children not live at home during Rumspringa if they were going to flaunt their bad behavior. Afterward, if their children decided against joining the church, many of these stricter families cut off all contact with them. These parents were raised to believe "you'd be better off losing a child through death than having him not be baptized." It was an extreme way to feel but understandable, I guess. Their whole lives they'd been taught at church that their most important duty in life, after saving their own souls, was to raise their sons and daughters to be the next generation of Amish, carrying on the faith.

I was lucky. Even though my dad was a deacon, my parents were more tolerant than that. They actually believe the "free" part of free-will baptism, that a decision as important as this one really should be voluntary.

From the day their sixteen-year-old joins a youth group, many Amish parents start looking for signs of *unzufriede*, the Amish word for "discontent." Is he going on trips to far-off locations, too far for a horse-and-buggy? Is she hanging around with non-Amish friends? Is he taking a date to an English restaurant? More alarmingly, is he dating non-Amish girls? Is he suddenly interested in higher educa-tion, maybe even taking the GED or a class at the local community college?

I knew I'd been displaying plenty of *unzufriede*.

The adults around me had seen my sort of reluctance before. They didn't panic. My parents, my aunts and uncles and the other grown-ups at church, they understood that some young people, even devout young people—maybe even themselves back in the day— may need a little time to stretch and breathe. It was okay for young people to test their freedom, my folks believed, so long as it didn't become a permanent state of affairs. In their view, youthful freedom was meant to be a passing condition, kind of like voice-cracking or acne.

As I wrestled with the decision, I took some comfort in knowing that if I chose not to get baptized in the Old Order Church, I could still have a good relationship with my family. That was important to me.

If I'd been convinced, truly convinced, that the Old Older Amish rules were really the will of God, there'd have been no inner struggle. I would have been baptized freely in the Old Order Amish Church. I would have thrown away the car keys and said good-bye to my guitar, sent my regrets to the next band hop, found a nice Amish girl and given her the life she expected. But ultimately, I wasn't convinced. I came to see that my God was more open than my church was. As far as I could tell, the church was more dependent on the arbitrary decisions of men than anything that was coming down from heaven.

When I was truthful with myself, I knew that I'd been experiencing feelings of doubt from the time I was still a child. Those doubts never really died away. Maybe it was my natural sense of curiosity that got the better of me. But I was never truly satisfied with the explanations for the rules of the Ordnung. I had never stopped feeling Amish. I had never stopped knowing I was Amish. I will be Amish for the rest of my life. But after a lot of self-reflection, I came to believe that my version of being Amish—there are many, as I keep discovering—was leading me on a parallel but slightly different path. I decided to be baptized in the New Order Amish Church.

The New Order Amish are similar in many ways to the Old Order. They share the same history, tradition and culture and many of the same beliefs. But some of the interpretations are a little different. The most important difference is a greater tolerance for the secular world and a stronger emphasis on finding our own Amish ways.

This was the right answer for me. I could still be a genuine part of the Amish community I felt so close to. My parents would take comfort in the fact that I was baptized in a church they were familiar with that carried on many of the old traditions. But I could have the distance that allowed me to be truer both to the Amish community and to myself. In unexpected ways, I found that I could honor and protect the Amish even better with one foot outside my family's community. It gave me perspective, independence and the power of truth.

"If you don't want to be baptized in our church, find a good one," my mother had counseled me. I know she was relieved when I told her I had.

At age twenty-four, I was baptized in a beautiful ceremony at the Spring Garden New Order Amish Mennonite Church near White Horse in Lancaster County. Most, though not all, of my family was happy for me. All my sisters and brothers came that day. My mother and father seemed proud to be there by my side.

One of the other people who was baptized with me, a guy about my age, was at the church entirely alone. His Old Order family was so upset with him, they refused to attend at all. He seemed so lonely sitting there. I felt really bad for him.

The baptism ritual was exactly the same as the one used in Old Order churches. I'd been thinking about it since I was a boy. I knew the three questions by heart.

"Can you renounce the devil, the world and your own flesh and blood?" the bishop asked.

"Can you commit yourself to Christ and His church, and to abide by it and therein to live and to die?

"And in all order of the church, according to the word of the Lord, to be obedient and submissive to it and to help therein?"

The Amish don't dunk anyone in a lake like some religions do. But after three clear yeses to the three big questions, a deacon ladled water from a bucket into the bishop's cupped hands. The bishop let the water drip over my head. Then, with a ceremonial holy kiss, the bishop said a blessing and invited me, the newest baptized member, into the fellowship of the church.

I felt like I had made the hardest decision of my life, and I'd made it right.

PART II
MAKING OUR STAND

CHAPTER 8
FAIRY TALE

Who cares about the Amish?

For a good long while, hardly anyone in America did, which was perfectly fine with the Amish. They hadn't come to America seeking attention. They'd left Europe hoping to avoid it. But as time rolled on, more and more people began to hear the story of the peculiar religious communities where time almost stood still. People wanted to see this firsthand. The good news for the Amish was that curious visitors didn't come to drown them or torture them or throw them into jail. Mostly, the visitors just came to stare.

And come they did, by the millions. Today, more than twenty million visitors descend each year on a handful of Amish communities in Pennsylvania, Ohio, Indiana and other states. Eleven million of these visitors will find their way to Lancaster County, which has remained the center of gravity for Amish American life, even though Holmes County, Ohio, actually has a slightly larger Amish population. These visitors arrive by tour bus, family car and airplane from across America and around the world. They include families with children, older couples, college students, church groups—you name it, they come.

Those of us who live in Amish Country grumble about the cluelessness of tourist hordes, the way people in tourist areas always complain. We roll our eyes and joke to each other, "You think they'd like to come and watch me pull weeds from the garden? Maybe they'd like to help!" Then we thank our lucky stars the visitors keep coming and pray to God they will never grow tired of us. They eat in our local restaurants—fast food and slow food. They sleep in the area's chain motels. The visitors explore re-created Amish villages and go on endless house tours. They sample handmade chocolates and many kinds of pie. They drive the country roads and look for horse-and-buggies. (They don't always remember to slow down.) They patronize local tour companies and—this is the latest thing—spend hours at high-priced new-age spas, where they are rubbed, buffed, soaked and steamed to the smell of sassafras and the sound of wind chimes. Not my thing, but I hear it's relaxing. They bargain-hunt at giant outlet malls out on the highway, immediately forgetting the Amish lessons they just learned about the dangers of rampant materialism. They haul their squealing children to popular water parks. Before they head back to wherever it is they came from, many of them pick up a jar of apple butter or a loaf of fresh-baked bread or, if they're feeling a little flusher, maybe a hand-sewn Amish quilt or a smaller "quillow." Some creative types might snag an old farm implement—a nicked-up rake or a hoe or a pitchfork—to display as an art piece back home. In a thousand different ways, these visitors do what they can to soak up the unique story of the Amish while also squeezing in some more conventional American-vacation fun.

God bless 'em all! They see a unique part of the country, experience something different from what they're used to and leave a lot of money behind. Really huge of piles of money.

The economists put the figure at more than $2 billion a year. That's billion with a "b." Coming to see the Amish is the biggest thing going in these quiet rural towns. And the business of Amish tourism keeps growing every year.

Since *Amish Mafia* and the other knockoff shows came on television, there's been a whole new wave of interest in the Amish. People are traveling from farther than ever and staying longer and spending more. They keep asking, "Where's Levi?" and "Is Merlin really as scary as he seems on TV?" (The answers, just so you'll know, are "I'm around" and "yes.")

I can almost guarantee you that the tourist count, in dollars and in bodies, will be even higher next year. I'm certainly no economist, but I can see the cars at the Lincoln Highway Travelodge in Strasburg and the lines outside the Shady Maple Smorgasbord on Toddy Drive in East Earl. There's no denying the obvious: An awful lot of people are making an awful lot of money off the heartwarming story of the Amish.

I know this much: Those tourists aren't coming just for the Grand Slam breakfast at Denny's on Columbia Avenue. They're coming to see *us*. They could just as easily OD on cholesterol at home. If it weren't for the powerful lure of the Amish, downtown Lancaster would be a ghost town. The busy Park City shopping mall would be about as empty as Boyd Cemetery on a moonless night, and all those tourists would be hanging around Branson or Orlando or, I don't know, maybe the Jersey Shore. *Where's Snooki!*

• • •

It would be nice if a few more of those Amish-tourism dollars ended up in Amish hands. Some days it seems like the Amish are the only people who aren't making money off the popularity of the Amish. The Amish are little more than extras in someone else's movie— baling hay, picking tobacco, driving buggies and growing beards— while people they hardly know sell the tickets and keep the receipts. Put it like this: The Amish are less the beneficiaries of Amish tourism and more the bait.

The Amish don't own Wendy's franchises. They don't even own most of the restaurants serving "Amish" food. They don't run conference centers or family-style motels. They certainly aren't administering the loofah scrubs in the high-priced new-age spas. They don't drive tour buses or staff the chamber of commerce. They're back on their farms, plowing their fields and ducking tourists with cell-phone cameras. They do operate a few farm stands.

Some of those tourist businesses are operated by Mennonites, whose rules about mixing with outsiders and benefiting financially are looser than those of the traditional Amish. And some of the "Amish" crafts sold in the "Amish" craft stores are made by actual Amish craftspeople. Those people get paid. Some Amish construction crews are hired to build new stores and houses that the tourist boom has created a demand for. That's paying work. But the vast majority of these tourist-fueled businesses are owned and run by people whose main connection to the Amish is, well, that that's the lucky business they're in. They love the Amish the way a farmer loves his cow. He'd hate for someone to steal it, and he wants to keep the milk production high.

The tourism money goes mainly to non-Amish business owners and the Wall Street investors who control all those big national chains. Then some of that money trickles across the nearby communities in sales receipts and tax revenues, paying for fire protection the Amish seldom rely on, police departments the Amish rarely call and public schools the Amish don't send their children to.

The tourists themselves don't tune in to much of this. They are kept purposely in the dark. They have no easy way of telling if the quilt they just bought was sewn by Mrs. Hardcastle in Bird-in-Hand or by a sweatshop worker on the outskirts of Shanghai. And either is perfectly possible. (Here's a hint: If the tag on the "Amish hand-stitched quilt" features a super-bargain price, chances are the item isn't really Amish. A lot of time and work goes into the real ones.)

Even the giant tour companies that scoot guests around in minivans and walk them through the re-created Amish villages—hardly any of those businesses are Amish owned. Don't be fooled by all those Amish-heavy names. Amish Acres. The Amish Experience at Plain & Fancy Farm, Amish Heartland Tours. The Amish don't own those companies any more than Mickey owns Disneyland.

Tourism is a time-honored tradition in Amish Country. For almost as long as there have been Amish in America, there have been people coming to look at them. From the day they arrived, the Amish were different from most other people. They lived with their own unique customs. They worshipped in their own special ways. They weren't super friendly when strangers came calling, but they were friendly enough. They were a far cry from Appalachian moonshiners—another band of rural exotics—who tended to greet their curious visitors with shotguns and growling dogs. If the Amish seemed a little odd or offbeat—well, that was part of their charm.

There are scattered reports from the 1800s of visitors arriving in rural Pennsylvania and Ohio by stagecoach, eager to see the Amish. They came from places like Philadelphia, Boston and New York. Back then, horses were everywhere. So Amish buggies didn't stand out like they would in later years. In those pre-auto, pre-telephone, pre-electricity days, the Amish didn't live all that differently from most people—just differently enough to be interesting.

Slower, quieter perhaps and with very long beards.

It wasn't until the late 1930s that the earliest hints of an organized Amish-tourism industry began to take shape. The Great Depression still had Americans feeling frugal. A brewing world war had everyone on edge. When mothers and fathers took the big step of planning a family vacation, they tended to want a sensible, wholesome, not-too-distant place to go. Amish Country! So close and yet so far! The Amish were self-sufficient. They didn't depend on handouts, Wall Street or the banks. The Amish seemed unthreatening and quaint. And they were convenient. By train, bus or family automobile, their settlements were a few short hours from the largest population centers in the United States. Plus they weren't running off to war.

Much of America was doing just that, but the Amish are pacifists—they were registered conscientious objectors. As World War II ramped up, many young Amish men took advantage of farm deferments and stayed at home. Others were sent to civilian work camps where they wouldn't have to handle weapons, but they were ready to rejoin their families as soon as the war was done.

In those pre-Expedia, pre-Travelocity, pre-TripAdvisor days, travelers relied on printed tourist brochures. I wouldn't call them slick. One popular 1938 version—*The AMISH and the MENNO-*

NITES: A Study of the Social Customs and Habits of Pennsylvania's Plain People—was a wordy thirty-two pages, printed in black and white with no photographs. That pamphlet was as plain as the Amish themselves. The author was a Pennsylvania writer named Ammon Monroe Aurand Jr.—not Amish, of course, though he did have a full white beard and his name made him sound like something of a throwback.

"These Odd Folk Called Amish" was the title of chapter one. "ISN'T IT TRUE," Aurand wrote, "that the average person likes to know something odd or curious about the 'other fellow,' while assuming that there is little or nothing odd about himself?"

The rest of the pamphlet was more of a history lesson, but with supposed inside information and its own unique, can-you-believe-this plot twists. Aurand explained that the Amish are "severely plain" in the way that they live. "An informant," he wrote, "says that these people have no pictures on the walls—only mottos and gaudy calendars." He then attempted to lure families with promises of beautiful farmland. "The Amish and Mennonites are generally agriculturalists, which include grain, vegetables and that 'horrible weed' tobacco!"

For some reason, Aurand felt compelled to include his own speculation about how the Amish got that way and how they compared to other groups he described as "plain."

"Plain people," he wrote, "have numerous notions in common. It appears that they have little time for either Negroes, lawyers or rum. They also believe that bad fences (poorly kept) cause trouble between neighbors."

I'm not sure what other "plain people" he was talking about, but on the subject of Amish notions, I would say not all Amish feel that way. Personally, I have no problem with any people, no matter what race or occupation they come from. As for lawyers, I actually like mine, Todd Shill, very much. And as for rum, I like that even more than I like my lawyer.

I'm not sure anyone would have predicted that this early brochure would help kick off a multibillion-dollar tourist industry. But word did get around, and from that time forward, the numbers mostly kept going up. The only real dip came in the disastrous tourist year of 1979. Some of the problem came from Mother Nature. There were record-breaking rains that year. There were also fuel shortages and gas rationing. Traveling anywhere just seemed like a hassle. Then the real blow came. The nuclear reactor at Three Mile Island suffered a partial meltdown, the worst nuclear accident in American history. The plant was only twenty miles from Lancaster. The lieutenant governor, William Scranton III, suggested that residents stay indoors and farmers keep their animals under cover.

And if that weren't enough, national headlines also announced that year: "Polio Epidemic Strikes Amish Community." That was true. Though the church had no explicit policy against immunization, many large Amish families had decided to skip the polio vaccines because of the expense. Though polio was all but gone from America, eleven cases of the deadly virus were reported among the Amish by the end of that year.

There were three million fewer visitors in 1979 than in 1978.

Ever since, it's been up-up-up for Amish tourism, some of the biggest jumps coming after *Amish Mafia* and its spinoffs hit the air. Really, how could tourists not want to visit the land of beards, bonnets and yours truly?

CHAPTER 9
SHUN THIS!

My brother Christian got shunned, and it was partly on account of me. Okay, *mainly* on account of me. I felt terrible when it happened, and I swore I'd get him out of it—even if I had to play outside the traditional Amish rules.

Christian is five years older than I am. He's a hard worker, an excellent brother and a very good guy. Unlike me, he was baptized in the Old Order Amish Church. He and I had a business together building decks on peoples' houses and doing roofing jobs. Farming and construction—those are the two main choices for Amish people, the ones who aren't churning butter at an "Amish" tourist village or selling hand-stitched quilts and shoofly pies. When no one's educated past eighth grade, what do you expect us to grow up to be? Computer programmers? NASA engineers? Chris and I had C & L Siding and Treated Decks. You learn a thing or two about good construction when you raise a few barns. We made some really nice decks. Every morning, I would leave the house to pick up Chris. Then, I'd drive us to the job site in our beat-up Chevy work truck.

Now, everybody knows the Amish frown on motor vehicles. If you need to go someplace that's too far to walk, take the horse-and-buggy. But if it's too far for the horse-and-buggy, don't go. If it's somewhere you really want to go or really need to go, you're supposed to hire an English taxi driver. Let *him* risk eternal damnation for hauling you around. But here's a dirty little secret about the Amish, something outsiders aren't supposed to know. Even after Rumspringa, lots of Amish people own and drive cars. That's right. There are Amish who've been baptized who have both a family buggy and a family car. They leave the car at a neighbor's house or hide it in a field somewhere. They won't drive to church on Sunday or throw their forbidden driving into the bishop's face. But they still drive.

Driving, even if everyone knows you've been doing it for months or years, even if a lot of other people are doing it, can ruffle some feathers. And that's exactly what happened. Chris and I had gone to work in the truck as usual, but suddenly there was trouble.

One of Chris's Amish neighbors, a brushy who had a farm across the road, spied us driving to work. Brushies are what the Amish call married men, who start growing a beard right after their wedding day. Amish men aren't even supposed to trim or shape their beards once they take a wife. So, ladies, if he's sporting scruffy facial hair, he's taken—don't even think of making a fuss over him.

Well, this particular brushy—Alvin is his name—had been sitting out on his porch with his binoculars, staring across the road at us. Nobody's as nosy as the Amish are. Without TV, radio and social media, sometimes folks go looking for their own drama. For some Amish people, binoculars are even more popular than cars. Binoculars and even telescopes are not banned by the Amish. I've known a lot of nice families who use them to bird-watch, and I've known just as many who use them to neighbor-watch. Brushy Alvin saw what he saw and probably didn't take the time to even put his binoculars back in their case before he went running straight to Bishop Fisher. I bet their conversation went something like this:

"The Stoltzfus brothers are driving," the brushy probably whined. "That's not right. You have to do something."

"Levi's not even baptized in the Old Order Church," the bishop might have answered. "What do you want me to do?"

"But Chris is," Brushy Alvin would have immediately shot back. "It's not right that Chris is driving with Levi. Levi should know better, and if he doesn't know better, Chris should."

"It's his brother." Bishop Fisher now trying to calm my nosy neighbor. "It's for work. This isn't the worst thing that ever happened."

"It's still not right," the brushy must have insisted, refusing to give an inch of ground. "He's risking a shun."

Technically speaking, Brushy Alvin was right. Since Chris was baptized Old Order Amish, he shouldn't have been riding with me. It would have been fine if he'd ridden with an English taxi driver or anyone else who wasn't from an Amish family. But not this. Brushy Alvin seemed hell-bent on getting the bishop to act.

"All right," the bishop would finally say. "I'll see what I can do."

Meidung. That's the word in Pennsylvania Dutch for shunning. Literally, it means "avoidance." Like many parts of being Amish, shunning comes straight out of the Bible—in this case, from a lit-

eral reading of two verses in the New Testament. The main one is I
Corinthians 5:11. I call this the sin-is-thicker-than-blood verse. For
the sake of religious purity, it has created painful divisions in many
families over the years. In that Bible passage, Paul is telling the Corinthians that they should keep their distance from "brothers" who
have committed certain sins.

Warns Paul: "But now I have written unto you not to keep company, if any man that is called a brother be a fornicator, or covetous,
or an idolater, or a railer, or a drunkard, or an extortioner—not even
to eat with such a one."

Bible scholars say the apostle recognized that unrepentant sinners might be a bad influence on the Christians. I am very familiar
with that theory as people have sometimes applied it, unfairly, to
me. Paul was also worried that if Christians hung around people who
were misbehaving, other people would think the Christians were no
better than the sinners they were with—just hypocrites preaching
one way and acting another. That's where the shunning comes in.

They were "not to keep company with these sinners . . . even to
eat with such a one."

The same shunning message is hammered home in Romans
16:17: "Now I beseech you, brethren, mark them which cause divisions and offenses contrary to the doctrine which ye have learned;
and avoid them."

Those in your life who are "contrary to the doctrine . . . avoid
them."

Originally, the Anabaptists were a little less harsh, but just a
little. They followed the principles of the Schleitheim Confession,
a statement adopted in 1527 by Michael Sattler, the leader of the
Swiss and German Anabaptists. In this statement, it was written

that "those who slip and fall into sin should be admonished twice in secret, but the third offense should be openly disciplined and banned as a final recourse. This should always occur prior to the breaking of the bread."

They banned sinners but not eating together.

Maybe one of the reasons that rule didn't stick was that soon after Sattler officially adopted it, he was arrested by Austrian Roman Catholic authorities. After a quick trial, he was executed.

Jakob Ammann, always among the strictest Anabaptist leaders, preferred the Dordrecht Confession of Faith, written in 1632. The seventeenth article is very clear: "Concerning the withdrawing from, or shunning the separated, we believe and confess, that if any one, either through his wicked life or perverted doctrine, has so far fallen that he is separated from God, and, consequently, also separated and punished by the church, the same must, according to the doctrine of Christ and His apostles, be shunned, without distinction, by all the fellow members of the church, especially those to whom it is known, in eating, drinking, and other similar intercourse."

Ammann's followers were taught that Christians must not associate at all with sinners who refuse to repent—even close family members. Not even to share a meal. The consequences of that, we have learned in the centuries since, can be enormous. From those two lines of tough love in the Bible to the interpretations of the confessions, families have been fractured, feelings have been hurt, countless lives have been ruined.

That brings up a huge issue—the whole question of interpreting what is a sin. Other religions struggle with the meaning of scripture, but not the Amish. It is as it is written, and that's that.

But hold on a second!

What do the Amish bishops and preachers know?

How do these Amish Bible experts know the real meaning of the Bible? How do they even know what the Bible says? I ask this because there isn't just one version of the Bible. There are hundreds. And they use different words in different languages to say different things. Which words are the true ones? And what's their true meaning?

This might not matter so much for religions that are inspired by the Bible or take broad themes from the Bible. The issue can be crucial, though, for a religion where words of the Bible can be—must be!—taken literally.

Okay, which words?

It turns out there are no easy answers to any of this. For one thing, the Bible wasn't written in Pennsylvania Dutch or English, the two languages most Amish people speak. I looked this up to be sure. I found out that the Old Testament was written first in Hebrew. I guess I remember learning that in school. Anyway, by the third century, the Old Testament was translated into Greek. By the fifth century, it was translated into Latin. As time went on, it was translated into many other languages, including English and many forms of German—but oddly, not Pennsylvania Dutch. The New Testament was written in Greek. Like the Old Testament, the New was translated into many other languages over the centuries—though again, not Pennsylvania Dutch. In most Amish homes and churches, you'll find the Gothic-script High German Bible. That version was translated into German from Hebrew and ancient Greek in the early 1500s by Martin Luther, the German friar and theologian whose criticism of the Catholic Church helped to spark the Protestant Reformation and inspired what is today the Lutheran Church.

There have been many, many translations of the Bible since the mid-1400s, when the first book ever printed was a Bible written in Latin. With each translation into another language, the writers took various liberties and used different words, which often have very different meanings. Bible experts are constantly arguing, even today, over which translations are more and less accurate. For the Amish, the debating has always started and ended with what is on the written page of the Bible they've chosen to use.

One fresh development has been stirring up a lot of interest lately. Amish-born Hank Hershberger and his wife, Ruth, spent twenty-five years in Australia, where they translated Bibles for the Gugu-Yalanji Aboriginal people. One day, Hank started thinking about the Bibles he'd been brought up with back home. They were Luther's Bibles, written in German. That's when he realized he'd never seen a Bible written in Pennsylvania Dutch.

He was inspired immediately. "The Lord seemed to tell me," he said, "'Your own folks don't have the Scriptures in their own language.'"

He and his wife got busy. In 2012, they finished translating both the Old and New Testaments into the language most Amish speak at home and in church. You'd have thought that Amish church leaders would have immediately substituted the Pennsylvania Dutch version for the one they'd been using (and that few people could read, anyway). The Hershbergers, after all, are highly respected Bible translators. And Pennsylvania Dutch was one of the last languages on Earth to get its own Bible, which is strange when you think about it since the people who speak Pennsylvania Dutch are so dedicated to every last word in the Bible.

Up to now, not too many Amish church leaders seemed very interested in using the new Pennsylvania Dutch Bible. "This is relatively new to them," Hank said not long ago when he was asked about his translation. "As a result, they view it somewhat with suspicion."

That's too bad, I think. Pennsylvania Dutch is not that close to High German, and that means words are open to misinterpretation. I'll give you one example: Martin Luther used a certain word, *gesegnet,* in his translation to mean "blessed." The same word is also used in Pennsylvania Dutch, but there it means "saved." The confusion over this one word is very important to the Amish. It's where the whole idea of "works salvation," getting to heaven by doing good works, comes from.

Says Hank: "Instead of 'blessed are the people,' it means 'saved are the people' who do so-and-so, for theirs is the Kingdom of God." It might sound like a small difference. But when every syllable is carefully measured and turned into rules, no difference is small. Wouldn't it be better, if you're going to follow the word of God as closely as the Amish are supposed to, to understand exactly what the words say?

I don't know, maybe some shunning could be avoided that way.

When I heard about Brushy Alvin ratting us out to the bishop, I marched straight over to the nosy neighbor's house and confronted him.

"Why can't you leave us alone?" I demanded.

He knew as well as I did that lots of Amish people were driving cars. And believe me, they were going a lot more places than just to work. Brushy Alvin and his binoculars must have seen me coming across the field. He had an answer ready for me. Three or four answers, really.

"It's wrong," he said. "You shouldn't be driving your brother."

"That's my family, not yours," I told him. "Why don't you mind your own business?"

"My kids grow up," he said, "and they're gonna see this, and they're gonna want to drive, too. That's not right."

He backed that up, as the Amish often do, with a snappy proverb. "We pass our convictions to our children by the things we tolerate," he said.

"Your kids do everything they see other people doing?" I shot back at him. "Is that how you raise your children? Maybe you should worry more about your own family and stop worrying so much about us."

He just looked at me. He didn't say anything else. He didn't have to. He had the Ordnung on his side.

It was a typical Amish squabble. Amish people may seem humble and reluctant around outsiders, but it's a whole different story when we are with our own. We're expressing opinions, pointing fingers, trading insults and turning quickly judgmental.

I was angry. No one likes a rat, and no Amish like being reported to the bishop. There was no doubt that Brushy Alvin now knew how I felt about his sticking his nose in my business. I didn't let things get any more emotional. I just stormed away, grumbling beneath my breath.

Amish can be stubborn. So even though he didn't say the words, even though he believed he was right, I walked away thinking I had persuaded Brushy Alvin.

I told Chris I'd managed to quiet the busybody brushy. "We can keep driving like we always do," I assured my brother. "I don't think we'll hear any more out of him."

Ah, not quite.

The next thing I knew, Chris was being shunned over riding with me in the devil's Chevy truck.

I don't think Bishop Fisher wanted to do it. I know my father didn't, but our neighbor hadn't backed down at all, and the bishop must not have thought he had a choice. So he summoned my dad, who was still a deacon in the church, and told him all about Alvin and Chris and me and the truck.

My father already knew about our driving to work, and he didn't care as long as we didn't call attention to ourselves. But now Brushy was causing a ruckus. My smart-mouthed comments had probably made things worse. And the bishop was coming down on my dad, who, being a deacon, really didn't have much choice but to come down on Chris.

"I guess we'll have to shun you," my dad said to my brother. You could hear the pain in his voice. I could tell he didn't like the idea any better than Chris did.

My own brother! Shunned! For something as trivial as riding to work with me!

It seemed so ridiculous, but shunned he was.

The rules of *Meidung* are very specific and very clear. Church members are required to make the shunned understand he has forfeited his place in the Amish fellowship. He isn't "one of us" anymore. He doesn't belong. The shunning is supposed to be enforced by the person's neighbors, coworkers, friends and, worst of all, family—*everyone*. Amish are polite, of course, so no one has to say anything openly hostile. Church members aren't expected to confront or abuse or beat the shunned or cut their beards off. But in a community where belonging is as important as it is to the Amish, a physical beating might be more pleasant. For people who've always lived in a big, tight-knit community, poorly equipped for life outside, being shunned can be a horrible, horrible experience. But it's the method the Bible supposedly dictates to deal with those who break rules, big or small. Justice is rarely a big consideration, any more than balance is.

The shunned can still live at home with his family—where else would he go?—but even there the contact is tightly controlled. They can speak with each other when absolutely necessary, but that's about it. Families have no choice but to shun the person by not even eating at the same table.

The purpose of shunning is not to be cruel. That might be the result, but it's not the purpose. Shunning is meant to redeem the sinner. It's meant to make the person change—quit sinning, seek forgiveness, do what it takes to get back into the good graces of the church, the community and God. It is a very high-pressure tactic, which makes it a powerful one, at least initially.

I've been around quite a few people who've been shunned over the years. Maybe that says something about the friends I keep. But even for those who pretend not to care, it is very lonely to be shunned.

When my brother Chris was shunned, these rules applied. He lived in a house with his wife and two small daughters. Often, they came to our house for dinner. But none of us was supposed to talk directly to him. When it was time for supper at his own house or ours, he could stay in the same room, but he had to eat alone at a little table off to the side. No one was allowed to hand anything directly to him. If he wanted us to pass him the vegetables, we had to set them down first. Only then was he allowed to touch the bowl. Shunning was uncomfortable for everyone, but what else could we do?

There's no getting around it: Whatever the stated purpose of shunning—redemption?—the practice is still deeply humiliating. And also hugely effective. Shunning is what Amish parents hold over their children, the harshest threat of all. It's how the Amish church keeps people in line.

Chris's shunning seemed especially unfair to me. Lots of other Amish were driving all over Lebanon and Lancaster counties. Why should Chris get singled out? Just because of one busybody with binoculars who couldn't control his own children? Now our family had to pay?

I felt guilty. I knew the answer to "Why Chris?" was mostly his association with me.

My brother didn't argue with my dad or the bishop. He didn't complain at all. He just ate silently at the side table in the dining room and moped around the house. I could tell it was wearing on him. Shunning is isolation warfare, separating the sinner from the group. It says sternly: "As long as you keep on sinning, we won't talk to you. We won't respect you. You won't be part of this family. You are all but dead to us." I felt terrible, and I wasn't alone. It was also killing my father that we were shunning Chris.

He knew how dumb the whole thing was.

Chris couldn't wait to get to work in the morning, where it was just him and me and things could be relatively normal again. When he was at our house, I did what I could to make Chris feel better. I whispered to him every chance I got. "We'll get you out of this some-how," I said. "We'll figure something out."

And we did.

In order to end a shunning, you don't just have to persuade your family. An official Amish shunning is in the hands of the preachers and the bishop. You have to meet with the preachers on three sepa-rate Sundays. In that time, you have to convince them that you are truly, truly sorry for the sin you have committed—whether it's mur-der, doing bad things with the livestock or riding in an inappropriate vehicle—promising never, ever to commit that sin again. Only then can the shun be lifted.

That's what the rules say, anyway. Then there's the approach that Chris and I dreamed up. I wouldn't call it extortion. Let's just say I offered not to shine a headlight on a bad case of hypocrisy.

It was low, I know. But it was effective. Under the circumstances, I think it was the right thing to do.

I got word to the preachers that I wanted a meeting. I didn't think Chris's shunning was fair. My brother was riding to work with me in the morning, not on some crazy joyride. If the preachers didn't find a way to lift Chris's shunning, I announced, "maybe we should have a big public discussion about this whole driving thing—start naming a few names."

I knew the preachers wouldn't like that. Some of those names, I was certain, would hit close to home for them. If I had to, believe me, I could draw up a nice, long list.

I didn't plan to stop with the car drivers. There was plenty more hypocrisy to discuss. The prominent Amish business owner who'd been importing made-in-China blankets and calling them "Amish." The preacher's son who'd been keeping a red Corvette in the barn of a nearby English family. A red Corvette! And they were mad at Chris and me and our Chevy work truck?

"Which way are we going with this?" I asked one of the preachers.

"Don't be hasty," he pleaded. "I'm sure we can work something out." Turns out he was right, and an accommodation was reached that very afternoon. It was all laid out in a little script.

Chris went to see the preachers before church on Sunday. He told them he was very sorry for what he had done. He said he would hire a non-Amish driver, which he did—for exactly one day. No one asked what would happen the following day.

With that, the shun was lifted.

Everyone seemed relieved. The preachers shook Chris's hand, and then they hugged him. They told him they were happy to have him back in the fold. We rushed home together to share the news with our father. Even without cell phones or text messages, he had already heard. After using the English driver for one day, Chris climbed back into the work truck with me, and that's how we continued to get back and forth to work.

I'm not sure who told Brushy Alvin, but I'm pretty sure somebody did.

Every now and then, I still see him out on his porch with his binoculars. He's watching carefully, but he never said another word about driving again.

CHAPTER 10
WAY TOO CLOSE

A respected Amish father keeps seeking forgiveness for fornicating with his daughter—then keeps slipping back into her bedroom.

An Amish teen beds not just his cousin but a horse *and* a cow.

An Amish girl says that when her oldest brother finally stopped molesting her, her second-oldest brother stepped in—and her mother blamed *her*!

What is it with Amish guys and their sisters, their daughters, their cousins and the girl next door? What is it with Amish guys and their livestock? Are the back-road hormones that wild? Let me put this as delicately as I know how to: Some Amish families are much too close for comfort—and way outside the law.

Religious law or civil law, take your pick!

The Bible doesn't leave any room for doubt. Leviticus 18:6–18 includes a detailed roster of all the family members a child of God isn't supposed to have sex with: "You must never have sexual relations with a close relative, for I am the LORD. Do not violate your father by having sexual relations with your mother. She is your mother. You must not have sexual relations with her. Do not have sexual relations with any of your father's wives, for this would violate your father. Do not have sexual relations with your sister or half sister, whether she is your father's daughter or your mother's daughter, whether she was born into your household or someone else's. Do not have sexual relations with your granddaughter, whether she is your son's daughter or your daughter's daughter, for this would violate yourself. Do not have sexual relations with your stepsister, the daughter of any of your father's wives, for she is your sister. Do not have sexual relations with your father's sister, for she is your father's close relative. Do not have sexual relations with your mother's sister, for she is your mother's close relative. Do not violate your uncle, your father's brother, by having sexual relations with his wife, for she is your aunt. Do not have sexual relations with your daughter-in-law. She is your son's wife, so you must not have sexual relations with her. Do not have sexual relations with your brother's wife, for this would violate your brother."

The passage goes on and on like that, listing just about anyone who'd have any excuse to appear at the next extended-family reunion. The message is unmistakable. Do not do it with anyone but your spouse, and that rules out incest and adultery.

Nonetheless, it's the dark, dirty secret of Amish family life, the volume of unsanctioned sexual activity that keeps occurring. Actually, it's not even that big a secret. You won't read much about it in the *Budget, Die Botschaft* or the *Amish Country News*—and certainly not in the shiny tourist brochures. But these forbidden pursuits are a relentless topic of Amish Country whispering. I've known people, heard talk and seen it in my own extended family. It's never pretty. Everyone knows someone who did something they shouldn't have out behind the barn. Any thorough tour of the Amish experience can't possibly skip the perverted stuff.

Let me tell you: There's an unholy lot of it to choose from. Brothers and sisters, fathers and daughters, mothers and sons, people and livestock—it's hard to know even where to begin. And don't get me started on door handles, horse tackle and rolling pins. The strange Amish couplings are limited only by the imaginations of people with little practical experience and too much time on their hands.

There are no good statistics on the frequency of unsanctioned Amish sex. How could there be? Amish boys don't alert the bishop every time they slide into their sisters' bedrooms. Amish teens don't check in on Foursquare when tiptoeing into a horse stall late at night, even the ones who are secretly trolling the Internet. The state might have data on those who get caught, but the church keeps no registry of Amish pedophiles. Still, I can say this much without any fear of contradiction: When a religion treats normal sex like a guilt-laden obsession, natural human desires will come out in all kinds of twisted ways. There are God-fearing Amish who follow the Ordnung every day of their lives. Then there are people like Chester Mast.

A twenty-six-year-old Amish father of two from Curryville, Missouri, whose wife was pregnant with their third child, Chester Mast was accused of sexually assaulting six girls, one of them his cousin, in a case that thrust the insular Missouri Amish community into an unwelcome public spotlight. Over the years, Chester was said to have abused girls aged five to fifteen.

What was unusual about his case wasn't the accusations. Lots of Amish men have been accused and found guilty of things like that. What was unusual was that the claims finally ended up in regular criminal court. That doesn't happen as a matter of course. The elders in the Pike County Amish community had done everything they could to prevent the English world from interfering in what they considered a church matter. They'd excommunicated him several times over a period of six years as Chester moved around, giving him years to rack up fresh victims along the way.

"We've seen this coming for years," said Noah Schwartz, one of Chester's uncles. "The church worked desperately to get behind him, but it was a lost cause. I don't think we realized the seriousness of the crimes."

"We tried to work with it ourselves," said Joseph Wagler, the bishop for a neighboring church. "We punished him, and he owned up to it." But Chester just kept sinning. The Amish elders say they excommunicated Chester at least three times: in 2004 when he returned to Missouri amid accusations that he'd raped a cousin in Wisconsin, in 2009 after a new round of allegations surfaced and again in 2010, when the bishops had a lengthy debate among themselves and finally called the police. That almost never happens with the Amish, no matter how serious the crime.

There's a lot to be said for the Amish spirit of forgiveness: forgive, forget and move on. But while that may work when someone is accused of petty theft, there's also no doubt in my mind it's a whole different story when someone is committing serious, ongoing crimes. How many horrible things happen to innocent people while church elders wait around for the bad guy to repent, making a conscious decision not to get the law involved?

It's a troubling question, and the answer is depressing.

Once they knew what happened, the police questioned Chester. He denied everything at first, but he finally pleaded guilty at the

Pike County courthouse to charges of felony statutory rape, statutory sodomy and sexual misconduct involving a child. He was sentenced to fourteen years in prison. Later, he also pleaded no contest in Wisconsin to repeated acts of sexual assault on a child.

And the investigators, knowing the Amish predilection to keep things private, still aren't sure that covers everything. "There is still the thought that there are other victims out there," said Sergeant Sean Flynn of the Pike County sheriff's department, the lead investigator in the Missouri case.

Many of Chester's relatives stuck by him all the way. He just needed repentance and forgiveness, they said. Prison was a waste of energy and time. "No sin is so bad that you can't recognize it and take total responsibility," said his uncle Noah. After all, what mattered was Chester's heart—not the length of his confinement. "We're concerned that Chester is honest, not how many years he gets. If he lies and gets out of prison, then he's still a prisoner to his own self."

There is nothing, no matter how innocent or how heinous, that can't be forgiven at church—sometimes over and over again. That might make sense for some kinds of sins, but for something as deeply perverted as incest or rape, that's just wrong. There's always the simple "I slept with my neighbor's wife" and also the "I went to town and hired a prostitute," but then there's the hard-core stuff. The Amish often have trouble telling them apart. People are constantly confessing some perversion, then going on to commit it again.

What's incredible, even to someone like me who was raised Amish, is that in the rare instances that these cases end up in regular court, the judges often bend over backward being sympathetic to the Amish defendants. They figure the Amish have it covered. Take nineteen-year-old Christian G. Stoltzfus of Fennimore, Wisconsin. He was arrested in 2010 for a laundry list of sleazy sexual acts that he was accused of committing over a four-year period on Amish farms in Hickory Grove and Mount Ida.

According to Grant County sheriff Keith Govier, the victims included at least six family members, a cow and a horse. Christian must have missed Bible study on Leviticus 20 day: "If a man has sex with an animal, he must be put to death, and the animal must be killed."

After a three-month investigation by the Grant County sheriff's department and the Grant County Department of Social Services, Christian was buried in an avalanche of eleven sex-related criminal counts—incest, repeated sexual assault of a child, attempted first-degree sexual assault of a child under the age of thirteen without great bodily harm, exposing his genitals and sexual gratification with an animal—the horse and the cow.

While Amish having sex with animals is definitely something people talk about more than occasionally, it's far less prevalent than the other large perversion we have in our midst. Amish having sex with people in their own close family is something I've heard about so many times that, no matter what it says in the Bible, I don't know for sure that everyone thinks it is wrong. Believe me, it is wrong. Of this, I'm certain, and it's sad to me that with incest being the dark secret of the Amish family, far too many victims suffer in silence for years—sometimes for the rest of their lives.

No one should have to do that.

A large part of the problem is how strongly the Amish believe in handling these issues entirely inside the community—without police or social workers or anyone else from the outside world. The bishops might intercede. Someone might be briefly shunned and then quickly forgiven.

The case of Christian Stoltzfus is a good example. The judge must've thought Christian, with his horse-and-buggy ride, wasn't a flight risk. The court decided he did not have to wait in jail for his trial date. He was freed on a $1,000 signature bond. The only conditions were that he not have unsupervised contact with any children younger than eighteen or with any live animals. I guess he was supposed to walk everywhere.

The case kicked around the Grant County courthouse for a while. His family and the victims' families wrote to county circuit judge Robert VanDeHey, saying what a good guy Christian was and how sorry he felt. On March 29, 2011, Grant County prosecutors agreed to a deal, allowing Christian to plead guilty to lesser charges and putting his future in the hands of Judge VanDeHey.

Under Wisconsin law, the judge noted, Christian faced more than 250 years in prison. Then, instead of 250 years in prison, the judge gave Christian one year of work release. It was as far away as you could get from the death penalty the Old Testament lawgivers had called for—no prison time at all!

"It's difficult to not send you to prison," the judge fretted. But he said prison might not be a good thing—*for Christian*! "Sending you to prison would take away the outstanding support system" he had in the Amish community and might turn young Christian into "a much more dangerous person."

The victims' families weren't out for blood, the judge said. And the Amish community "took steps" to get him into treatment as a "safety plan."

Call it Amish justice, courthouse style!

Christian's eighteen-year-old-brother, Dannie, also received a similar rash of charges for molesting family members—though his case involved just a horse, no cows. He got a similarly gentle result: no jail time and no probation. But the brother was fined one hundred dollars and given sixty days to pay up. Or if that was impossible or too much trouble, the judge invited Dannie to set up a more convenient payment plan.

O ccasionally, outsiders try to help.

Prosecutors encourage victims to come forward and testify. Some battered-women's shelters try to get the word out: They are a safe haven for Amish women who need one. Concerned English neighbors occasionally offer a sympathetic ear. And there are good-hearted people like Judy Jonke of Ohio's Geauga County Domestic Violence Task Force, who passes out free purple-and-white paper cookbooks to Amish women around the community. *Recipes from an Amish Kitchen*, the books are blandly called, but scattered among the recipes for ham casserole and beefy barbecue macaroni is life-saving information on domestic and sexual violence.

That includes safety tips and phone numbers for local shelters and the county sheriff's office. "They're scared of the violence in the house and don't have a way out," Judy says of the Amish women she hopes to reach. "Men are the supporters. You listen to them. You don't say anything. It's a man's world."

If a husband happens to notice one of the special cookbooks, maybe he'll just think it's a cookbook. Chances are he wouldn't want to be caught leafing through a woman's recipe book.

With the old slap-on-the-wrist mentality, it's often the victims who are blamed. That's one of the reasons why it's extremely rare for Amish women to tell stories of sexual abuse to the larger world.

One who has spoken out is Anna Slabaugh. In an interview with *Dateline* on NBC, she says she was forced to endure years of sexual abuse by her brothers in Ohio Amish Country.

The eighth of nine children in an Ohio Amish family, she says she was sexually abused for years. It started with an older brother, when she was eleven and he was nineteen. "He dared me to touch him in an inappropriate way and also dared me to let him touch me," she said. "And I took up his dare."

It wasn't a one-time thing. She recalled being assaulted "at least once a week." "If I told him it hurt, he'd just call me a wimp." When that brother moved out of the house, her seventeen-year-old brother stepped in, often catching her in the family barn on Sundays after church. "He went much further than my oldest brother had," she said. "He wanted to do things. You know, he wanted to have intercourse and everything. And at that point, I was pretty sure that was wrong. For one, I was too little."

But he insisted, and she went along. That went on for a couple of years.

Anna might have felt her years of horror were finally over when her mother caught them one day. But, she recalled, her mother didn't punish the brother. She punished Anna. "I was locked in my room," she said.

She said she'd wanted to speak out when she was younger, but the cost was unthinkably high. Finally one day, Anna used a telephone in an English house she was cleaning to call a battered-women's shelter in Mount Vernon, Ohio. The counselors on the other end of the line didn't take her seriously at first. Anna couldn't give up. She needed help. After a month of relentless calls, the shelter finally alerted Knox County's Children and Family Services Division. A child abuse investigator spoke to Anna about her ordeal and alerted the police. But before detectives launched any kind of criminal investigation, Anna Slabaugh's family moved out of the state to Tionesta, Pennsylvania.

The abuse finally stopped there. But Anna said she still didn't feel safe with her family and was determined to leave. She told anyone who would listen, including a Pennsylvania state trooper, that she wanted to get away from her family, that she was too frightened to stay. Somehow, her family found out. Now they were steaming mad.

One day when Anna had a toothache, her mother took her to see an Amish dentist and the dentist yanked out all of her daughter's teeth. Even though she'd had just a simple toothache, now she had a full mouth of horrible pain. Toothless, she felt terribly disfigured. But her mother didn't express any sympathy. Recalled Anna: "After he had pulled the last tooth, my mom looked at me and said, 'I guess you won't be talking anymore.'"

Although the report to the state trooper prompted an invesigation, Anna says she recanted her story at a court hearing because she was so depressed and feeling so defeated from her prior efforts to speak out. So, no one has ever been convicted of sexually abusing Anna. Neither of her brothers had to stand trial. In fact, no formal charges were ever filed, although the young girl had sought help in two different states.

Anna finally made her break with the help of a friend's family. She spent the next two years with foster families. She finally feels safe, she says, but worries about her younger sister.

"I know that she's been beaten," Anna said of her sister. "She was when I was still there. But whether she's been sexually molested, I just pray to God that she hasn't."

CHAPTER 11
BUI

There's a T-shirt with a slogan I think is funny.

It shows the silhouette of an Amish man with hat, beard and suspenders and offers an excellent piece of advice: DON'T DRINK OR DRIVE, as if the Amish are always opposed to both.

There's a lot of confusion and misconception when it comes to alcohol and the Amish. Many people I've met seem to believe that the Amish aren't permitted to drink at all. That's not true. The Amish aren't Mormons or evangelical Christians or devout Muslims. Alcohol isn't the devil's nectar, as far as the Amish are concerned. Wine especially is all over the Bible. At the feast at Cana, Jesus didn't turn the water into chocolate milk.

It's *excessive* drinking or *inappropriate* drinking or *dangerous* drinking that conflict with key Amish values such as clearheadedness, personal responsibility and hard work. The occasional glass of wine at dinner is one thing. Getting loaded on Saturday night is something else entirely. You might have a hangover at church! I'm just waiting for someone to print up the Amish Country bumper sticker that says: FRIENDS DON'T LET FRIENDS BUGGY DRUNK!

I understand: The intoxicated operation of a horse-drawn carriage is just as dangerous as the intoxicated operation of a motorized one. Well, maybe not *just* as dangerous. Very few horses can gallop seventy or eighty miles an hour, even when you're late for church. And a horse-drawn carriage, by definition, has a horsepower of one, about one two-hundredth of the oomph of a typical American family car. But BUI, buggying under the influence, is still best avoided.

Believe me, I know. I've tried it. I've been caught driving a car under the influence, twice. But this happened in my buggy, and it wasn't pretty. One night, I went weaving past the Rail Road Diner on Race Street (I swear, that's the street name) near my house in Richland, too loaded to walk safely much less steer a carriage and a horse. I must have thought I was chasing Jeff Gordon at the Pocono Raceway. I just kept slapping the reins and shouting, *"Go! Go! Go!"* Thank God I was alone. It's hard enough maintaining control of a horse when everyone's stone-cold sober—the driver and the horse. I was lucky to get back home without being arrested or killing anyone.

I don't remember the ride back home at all. But every Amish kid knows that if you get drunk and fall asleep in the buggy, the horse will take you home. Somewhere in that horse brain is a foolproof GPS system. The only problem is it has only one destination plugged in: home. Always home. I proved it again that night. The horse must have known the way, because I sure didn't. I was still totally wasted when I stumbled into the house.

The first Amish guy I ever heard of getting arrested for buggying under the influence was Elmer Stoltzfus Fisher. Elmer was a young Amish carpenter in his early twenties. One Sunday evening in early December, he might have had a little too much Christmas cheer. He was heading back to his farm in Paradise.

A quick aside: Paradise is one of those Pennsylvania Dutch Country places whose name is fitting for a religious community, unlike Blue Ball, Bareville, Mount Joy and the always hilarious town of Intercourse, Pennsylvania, whose names make the tourist snicker, especially the tourists under ten years old. Paradise holds the special distinction of being the setting for a very funny 1994 Christmas-themed crime comedy called *Trapped in Paradise*, which starred Nicolas Cage, Jon Lovitz and Dana Carvey. I hear that Intercourse has been featured in some movies too, though I don't believe I have seen any of those.

Anyway, Elmer was at the reins of his buggy that night, moving very, very slowly along North Ronks Road, which is a two-way thoroughfare with cars whizzing by. He wasn't riding to the left. He wasn't riding to the right. He was creeping along the center line. I'm not sure if that was his decision or the horse's. Either way, the buggy wasn't difficult to catch up to.

Jesse Blank, an off-duty police officer in my hometown of Quarryville, happened to be driving by in his personal car. Sensing that something wasn't right, he slipped behind Elmer's buggy. Nate Perry, who was riding with the off-duty cop, jumped out and trotted alongside Elmer's slow-moving buggy. The young Amish man didn't seem to notice a thing, and no wonder. Through the window, Nate saw that Elmer seemed to be sleeping, slumped way down in the seat. The cop knocked on the buggy door—hard, several times. Only then did Elmer stir.

The off-duty cop called it in to the East Lampeter Township police, who reported to the scene. The incident report noted that Elmer and his horse had been "straddling the center line of the roadway." The responding officer detected a "strong odor of an alcoholic beverage" on Elmer's breath and noticed his "bloodshot, watery eyes." When Elmer took a Breathalyzer back at the station, he blew a .18 percent, more than twice the legal alcohol limit in Pennsylvania. On the official police report, the officer identified Elmer as the driver and, as well as he could, described the vehicle involved: "Year: NA [not applicable]. Model: NA. Make: HORSE & BUGGY." That might have happened elsewhere before this incident, but I'd never heard about it.

Elmer went quietly. Levi Detweiler, age seventeen, did not. In Leon, New York, a deputy from the Cattaraugus County sheriff's department observed Levi's buggy go through a stop sign without even slowing down. The moment the lights and siren went on, Levi and his horse took off. Rather than cooperate with his own arrest, Levi must have thought it wiser to take the police on an alcohol-fueled cruiser-buggy chase—a slow-speed chase from the officers' perspective, a very high-speed chase from the horse's. For a full mile, the cop stayed right behind the Amish speed demon. As the road turned sharply, Levi's buggy failed to negotiate the curve, ending up in a roadside ditch. That should have been the end of it, but Levi still wasn't ready to submit. He took off on foot, leaving the horse and buggy behind, with two deputy sheriffs in hot pursuit.

Levi didn't get far. He was grabbed, cuffed and charged with underage possession of alcohol, reckless endangerment, failure to stop at a stop sign and failure to yield to an emergency vehicle. He was driven, by car, off to jail.

"These cases aren't uncommon at all," says Steven Breit, a criminal-defense attorney who has represented quite a few Amish clients over the years. He's had BUIs, SUIs (scootering under the influence), HRUIs (horseback riding under the influence) and pretty much everything this side of butter churning under the influence. He also reps many non-Amish clients accused of normal DUIs.

Breit has made such a specialty of drunk-driving defense that he has printed up bar coasters with his name and phone number and distributed them to taverns across Lancaster and Lebanon Counties. Business got even brisker when Pennsylvania, like many states, lowered the drunk-driving threshold from .10 percent to .08 percent alcohol in a person's bloodstream. Just like in New York, the state put in a super-strict limit for anyone under the age of twenty-one, making it illegal to have an alcohol count even as low as .02. The Amish may not like mingling with outside legal authority, Breit says, but these days, police and prosecutors are perfectly happy sweeping up Amish drunk drivers along with all the rest.

"Back in the day," the lawyer says, "maybe the cop would just give a warning to the Amish buggy driver who'd had too much to drink, 'Just get on home, sir. Drive safely now.' But today, the police don't care if you're Amish or English or what you are. All these laws apply just as much to Amish teenagers and adults—during Rumspringa or coming home from a field party or just being out on a Saturday night."

There are some legitimate safety concerns. Even under the best of circumstances, buggies aren't that easy to see at night. Most of them are now outfitted with bright orange hazard triangles and flashing red safety lights. But the lights are battery powered. They're dim even when they are turned on. Because it's such a hassle recharging the batteries, some Amish buggy drivers turn off their flashing lights until they know someone's behind them. That gives hardly any warning before a car screeches up, and that's if they haven't been drinking too much to remember to flip the switch.

When it comes to drunk buggying, things are a little looser in some other states. In those places with fewer Amish on the roads, the vehicle has to be motorized before the drunk-driving laws apply. *Motorized* includes a lot—cars, trucks, SUVs, motorcycles, snowmobiles, motorboats and, if they're taken onto a public roadway, even riding mowers and golf carts. (And don't forget Dennis LeRoy Anderson's infamous drive home in a motorized La-Z-Boy. Police in Proctor, Minnesota, certainly haven't. Really, you can look this up under *CUI*—chairing under the influence.) In all those places, if the vehicle doesn't have a motor, the authorities have to make do with lesser charges such as disorderly conduct, public drunkenness or, in rare cases, reckless endangerment, if they can show the drunken buggier or bicyclist or scooter pusher is truly a danger to himself or others. Those offenses tend to carry lesser penalties than a normal DUI, and I don't think repeat offenders could be subject to Pennsylvania's habitual-offender five-year license-suspension law. No driver's license, no suspension, right?

But in several states with large Amish populations, Pennsylvania included, the drunk-driving laws don't even require that a vehicle be motorized. "In our state, the law applies to buggies, scooters, bicycles, tricycles, horseback, it doesn't matter," Breit says—damn near anything with wheels, blades or hooves. Drunk driving is drunk driving is drunk driving, and the handcuffs quickly come out.

Still, experienced defense lawyers do have a range of arguments they have learned to make on behalf of their Amish clients. They're not so different from the ones they make for the non-Amish. If the buggy hit a tree and there are no other witnesses, how do we really know what occurred? "There's a lot of things you can question," Breit says. "And how do we know the horse wasn't at fault? Horses can buck. Horses get spooked."

However, Breit says that so far, none of his Amish clients have wanted to blame the horse.

CHAPTER 12
COKE BROTHERS

Abner King Stoltzfus should have paid more attention. There were warnings all over the Bible, as there so often are when a nice young man is sliding down an obviously perilous path. How much plainer could 1 Corinthians have been? "The sacrifices of pagans are offered to demons, not to God, and I do not want you to be participants with demons."

Things started out innocently enough. Abner agreed to give a long-haired English guy a ride home. The Amish are neighborly like that.

Abner came from the close-knit Amish community in Gap, an old nickel-mine town in Lancaster County named for the nearby gap in the Appalachian Mountains. He was a thin twenty-two-year-old with curly, dirty-blond hair, a friendly young man five or six years into a fairly routine Rumspringa. He had his own company, AS Roofing. I don't believe he and I are close kin, though we do share middle and last names.

Lancaster County is crawling with people named Stoltzfus. You could say that *Stoltzfus* is the *Smith* or *Jones* of Pennsylvania

Dutch Country, but Smith and Jones don't hold a candle to Stoltzfus if we're just talking percentages. Nearly one-quarter of the thirty thousand Amish people in the Lancaster area are named Stoltzfus, and many, many more have Stoltzfus blood running through their veins. Genealogists say that almost all of us are descended from one man, Nicholas Stoltzfus, who came to Pennsylvania from Germany in 1766. Ben Riehl, a know-it-all farmer from Intercourse who tracks Amish heritage, was asked about Nicholas Stoltzfus's widespread impact. "It's even more than people realize," Ben said. He estimated that 98 percent of the Amish population of America descends from Old Nick. "If he hadn't made the decision to move over here, we'd all probably still be in Europe," Ben said.

Back to Abner. He and another Amish friend had driven out of the county to see a demolition derby, where they had a grand time watching perfectly good cars smash each other up. The hippie needed a ride, and the Amish are nothing if not polite.

It was in the car that their grateful passenger pulled out a small pipe.

"You want a little?" he asked.

After some brief reluctance, Abner and his friend each agreed to take a hit. It was pot, of course, and, of course, they liked it. By the time they crossed back into Lancaster County, Abner had agreed to buy a $20 bag.

That was his introduction to an element of modern American life that his strict Amish upbringing had mostly shielded him from. Apparently, this was not the case with every Amish kid. Weed, it turned out, had become quite popular with some Crickets, Antiques, Pilgrims and other Amish young people. The kids even had a special Amish name for the intoxicating weed: *green corn*.

Then things got really interesting. One day, a friend and fellow roofer from Gap whose name was also Abner Stoltzfus (no kidding, and also no close relation to the first Abner or to me—let's call him Abner Two) turned him on to the devil's white powder, cocaine. Like a character in a back-roads remake of *Reefer Madness*, he went spiraling into places he never even knew existed before. He discovered a far-flung subculture of fun-loving Amish druggies. Abner liked the coke even more than he liked the special green corn, and that was saying something. He liked the coke so much, in fact, he wanted more of it and more of it and maybe just a little more of it—*now*! In no time, the two Abners went to see a large, tattooed biker whose nickname was Juke.

"We went over to the guy's house," Abner would explain later to a writer from *Philadelphia* magazine. "I was scared. I thought, I don't want to be here. There was this big four-hundred-pound guy on the sofa, just looking at us. I was scared to death. What am I doing here?"

Buying coke was how the visit began. The coke-dealing biker Juke and his nearly-as-large friend Big Dwayne mentioned proudly that they ran with a motorcycle club called the Pagans. The Pagans, Juke and Big Dwayne added, had excellent connections in the world of illegal narcotics distribution—or words to that effect.

Despite the initial discomfort, everyone seemed to be getting along just fine. Juke apparently had worked a roofing job with Abner Two. They had that bond. And the bikers sniffed a unique business opportunity in their new Amish friends. Where some people viewed the Amish as distant, backward or impossibly devout, Juke apparently saw the younger generation of plain people as an untapped market for Pagan cocaine.

Nearing the end of their Rumspringa days, the Abners found a special role for themselves connecting two worlds, Amish youth and drugs. The real action, they knew, was at band hops and other large field parties where hundreds of Amish teens gathered under the stars for kick-your-shoes-off nights of laughing, singing, dancing, drinking and fun.

Once the Abners turned up with their special powder, those nights would include some heavy drugging, too.

A lot of outsiders were surprised that the Amish and the bikers connected so easily. I wasn't surprised. I've always gotten along well with bikers, whichever clubs they ran with. Like the Amish, bikers often work construction. They follow rules of their own. Like the Amish, they have their own cohorts and their own sense of style. They dress differently and talk differently and work differently from most other people. They aren't too concerned about what straight society thinks.

As it happened, the Abners were not very shrewd drug dealers. For one thing, they made a classic amateur mistake: They couldn't seem to decide if they were looking to make money or friends. They laid out piles of cocaine just as the young Rumspringa partiers were arriving. They didn't collect any money up front. They let their friends and friends' friends pay on the honor system for however much they used. Bad idea. That approach fell short of the Pagans' usual standards of inventory control. The Abners were moving six or seven thousand dollars' worth of coke some weekends—but they still had trouble keeping up with their supply bills.

As Abner said later: "I'd start drinking beer and lose track of who I gave to."

It didn't take long for the authorities to catch a whiff of this Amish-Pagan drug connection. The multistate motorcycle club, with sixteen chapters in Pennsylvania alone, had attracted plenty of police scrutiny over the years—and not just for their provocative name. Various members and associates had been accused of a wide variety of criminal activities—drug running, violent extortion, domestic abuse and many, many open-road traffic violations.

When state and federal undercover drug agents began hearing talk that the Pagans were reaching into the very heart of the Pennsylvania Amish community, the agents could hardly believe their ears. "Bikes and buggies—it's a rather strange combination," said Pennsylvania state police major Robert Werts. "Our drug investigations are taking us to places where years ago we didn't think we had a problem."

"It's something in my twenty-six years in the FBI I've never encountered before," agreed Robert Conforti, special agent in charge of the FBI's Philadelphia office. Yes, Amish teenagers sometimes referred to their youth groups as "gangs." But no one ever thought they meant the organized-crime kind.

The state police took the direct approach. Two troopers showed up at Abner's front door. The troopers explained that they were investigating a large-scale drug ring that two young Amish men were a small part of. No one had to shine bright lights in Abner's eyes or whack Abner Two with a rubber hose. Abner confessed immediately. Without much prodding, he agreed to wear a wire and record his next drug buy with the Pagans. He hid the little microphone in his black Amish hat, where even the famously paranoid bikers didn't think to look.

When the indictment was returned at the federal courthouse in downtown Philadelphia, it detailed a seven-year, $1 million drug-sale conspiracy that had involved the Amish for the final two years. The conspiracy allegedly began in 1992 when members of the Chester County chapter of the Pagans, joined by assorted "hang-arounds," started selling multikilogram quantities of powder coke and meth through the bars and taverns of Chester and Lancaster Counties.

Some weekends, it was said, the Abners sold just a couple of thousand dollars' worth. But sometimes, when the parties grew to five hundred people or more, the dollars went way higher than that. Eight-thousand-dollar nights were not unheard of.

Leading the Pagan conspiracy, the prosecutors said, was Emory Edward Reed, forty-seven, of Millersville, and his sergeant at arms Dwayne Blank of Gap. If the indictment was to be believed, Reed broke a fellow Pagan's leg with an ax when the man refused to follow an order. He allegedly knocked out another man's teeth when he was late in making drug payments.

What can you say? Abner should thank his lucky stars no one noticed his hat wire.

It had once been possible to deny that the Amish had a drug problem at all. George H. W. Bush, the first President Bush, came to Lancaster County in March of 1989 and did exactly that. He brought with him Attorney General Dick Thornburgh and the new White House drug czar, William Bennett. They met that day with a dozen Amish and Mennonite elders at the Penn Johns Elementary School in Bird-in-Hand. The president started on a cheerful note, declaring that he had come "to salute [the Amish and Mennonites] because as we look at a national drug problem, we find that in communities such as yours—because of your adherence to family values and faith—the problem appears to be close to nonexistent, hopefully nonexistent."

Really?

The president asked if anyone in the room could account for this complete absence of drugs in their world. A Mennonite man said he believed he could explain the phenomenon. "I think the fact that we have no trouble with drug addiction is because of the close family ties and the children are taught obedience at a very young age—and self-denial—that they don't have everything they wish as they're growing up," the man said. "And because they are taught of God and urged to pray, and in school have prayer and Bible reading. And as they grow up, they have a sense of value that they're not just out seeking thrills and drugs or any other."

President Bush said he couldn't agree more, suggesting maybe he'd found the solution to America's drug problems right here in Lancaster County. "I am absolutely certain," he said, "that family values and community and faith—where those abound, the problems that we're talking about of fighting narcotics, the fight is easier and the problem less big."

But others at the meeting didn't sound so sure. A couple of people said they'd already picked up signs that illegal drugs were creeping into their communities, too. One man said that his son had accepted a ride in a pickup truck and was offered marijuana. "It makes me almost quiver in my boots," the man said, "when I think that that youth could have been tempted to do that because he was exposed to it."

The drug czar, Bennett, tried to gauge the feelings in the room. "Are things better than they were five years ago? Are they worse than they were?"

Again, the doubts were raised. One man stood and said, "In my opinion, it would be worse because our two oldest sons work at public places and they both were exposed to drugs and had opportunity to buy."

Attorney General Thornburgh finally took the floor to remind everyone that the president was deeply committed to keeping communities like theirs drug-free. "President Bush, I'm sure you've heard it said, has established a goal of providing a kinder and gentler America. And I think that's one that we support to a man or woman throughout this country. But a kinder, gentler America is not one where drugs are abused and where drug traffickers rule the streets of some of our communities."

Of course, that turned out to be wishful thinking. President Bush's policies didn't cure America's drug problem, any more than any of his predecessors' had. And the Amish weren't living in total isolation. They'd find out that they weren't any more immune to drug abuse than people in any other community.

People in Amish Country seemed to get that eventually, much as they wish it weren't true. One Amish father, Ed Miller, told a reporter who came snooping around: "The devil doesn't care where we live, whether in the city or in the country. He seeks out the weakest."

Every group has its "weakest."

A year before the two Abners hit the headlines, an anonymous letter was circulated to Amish parents and youth, warning about the dangers of drug abuse. No one took public credit, but the language certainly sounded ominous. "Beware of the evil changes your children might be going through," the letter warned.

As requested, the letter was read aloud in Amish churches throughout Lancaster County. Clearly, the writers knew there was a problem and how pervasive it was. The letter specifically mentioned marijuana, cocaine and heroin, saying all three were available to their children. "May the Lord help us and grant us wisdom, strength and grace to work on this problem we have with some of our young people using drugs," the letter said.

It was signed, "With heavy hearts, Concerned Parents of Our Youth Today."

But the Amish are very private people, and while they were willing to address the problem among themselves, they weren't at all happy that this embarrassing episode was now very much in the spotlight. Suddenly, it seemed everyone was talking about the Amish tradition of Rumspringa and all the antisocial behavior it seemed to keep sparking. Church leaders were appalled that their quiet communities were being portrayed as places that tolerated drugs and partying—not just tolerated those evils but almost seemed to condone them. "It is a gross inaccuracy to talk about accepting the sowing of wild oats," said one bishop, who refused to allow his name to be used. "It's a small minority that everybody notices who does that. Ninety-eight percent never do."

There was no actual data, of course—but also no shortage of wishful thinking.

In a further attempt to distance his rule-abiding flock from the two Abners, the bishop reminded everyone that while they were raised Amish and were both active members of Amish youth groups, neither had yet been baptized. "These fellows are no more Amish than I am Nazi," the bishop said.

But what really got to the Amish wasn't just the news coverage. It was the merciless jokes, repeated night after night on network TV.

"What was the worst Amish crime until now?" Jay Leno asked an actor dressed as an Amish police chief. "Cow-jacking," the Amish chief replied to the uproarious laughter of the *Tonight Show* audience.

David Letterman devoted one of his famous Top Ten Lists to "signs your Amish teen is in trouble." Most of the Amish people in the area didn't see the show when it aired on CBS on June 24, 1998, any more than they'd caught Jay Leno's skit. Despite the cracks in Amish isolation, most homes were still not equipped with televisions. But a local newspaper printed Letterman's whole, painful list of Amish-teen trouble signs.

"In his sock drawer, you find pictures of women without bonnets."

"When you criticize him, he yells, 'Thou suck!'"

Number five was: "Defiantly says, 'If I had a radio, I'd listen to rap.'"

The list wrapped up with:

"He was recently pulled over for 'driving under the influence of cottage cheese.'"

And "He was wearing his big black hat backwards."

Soon enough, even local people were joking about the case. You couldn't go to town without overhearing something. "Did you hear the one about the FBI agents? They're stopping in at Amish coffee breaks and making sure the white powder on the doughnuts isn't cocaine."

Or "Did you hear they're filming a sequel to *Witness*? It's called *Defendant*."

It wasn't that the Amish had no sense of humor, they kept telling one another, but couldn't all the jokesters go pick on someone else?

Whe the Abners' case finally got to court, their defense lawyers pleaded addiction and Rumspringa. Those weren't the official defenses, but they might as well have been. What else could the defense lawyers argue? The police had all the evidence they could possibly have wanted, and both the Amish defendants had confessed. Not only confessed, they'd cooperated with the police investigation of the others. "It was pretty clear" Abner Two had been addicted to cocaine, his lawyer, John Pyfer, said at the men's arraignment. During Rumspringa, the lawyer argued, Amish youth are expected to "sow their wild oats." During that time, he said, the young people are expected to drink and drive "bright, gaudy cars" while "their parents are looking the other way." Snorting cocaine is not an accepted part of that, the lawyer admitted. "We've seen plenty of underage drinking cases but a drug case is unheard of," he said.

Lawyers for the Pagans scoffed at the idea that the Abners were any different from their big, bad, motorcycle-riding alleged codefendants. "They're making the Amish out to be pristine, untarnished young men, corrupted by the evil Pagans," said Juke's lawyer, Hope Leferber. "The truth be known, these kids are the same as any other kids who surrender to the temptations of youth. They weren't corrupted. At best, they were willing participants."

There was no trial. How could there be? The evidence was so overwhelming. Everyone pleaded guilty—the Pagans, the Amish, the hang-arounds. The best they could do, they all decided, was to let their lawyer plead with U.S. District Court judge Clarence New-comer for mercy at sentencing time.

And the defense lawyers began to do just that.

"It just shows you that the same temptations that are out there for your kids and my kids have found their way into Amish life," said John Pyfer. "We're just glad they were able to nip this in the bud."

Obviously, this particular bud had flowered already.

"I can tell you my client wasn't driving a Cadillac or living the lifestyle of a drug dealer," the lawyer added. "Unfortunately, once you get a taste of cocaine, you have to satisfy it."

Judge Newcomer gave the stiffest sentence, eighty-four months, to Lawrence "Twisted" Mellot, who admitted distribut-ing meth and coke at bars in Chester County. The two men who'd brought the Abners in got off a little lighter. Juke, real name Doug-las Hersch, got sixty-three months. "Big Dwayne" Blank received fifty-five months, though his weight, which at sentencing tipped the scales at just over four hundred pounds, would make prison time especially challenging for him. Emory Edward Reed, the chapter president, was now cooperating with the authorities and hoping for a lighter sentence.

When sentencing day finally arrived for the two Abners, it was anything but normal at the federal courthouse in Philadelphia. The Abners and their lawyers and their immediate families were joined by three hundred Pennsylvania Amish, who made the long trip to the courthouse in a fleet of rented vans. The room was packed with men in black and women in long dresses. A court clerk asked the Amish men to remove their hats. The women all kept their bonnets on.

Before the judge announced the sentences, the federal prosecutors spoke. The two young Amish men, they said, had helped authorities crack the Pagan drug ring. This didn't absolve the Abners from guilt entirely, the prosecutors said. The young men had, in fact, moved something on the order of $100,000 worth of cocaine.

Then the Abners' supporters got a chance to speak. For nineteen minutes, people stood and praised both of them and all the good works they'd done since getting arrested. Friends told how the Abners had turned their lives around. An FBI agent said the pair had taken risks to help investigators. "They were scared to death," Special Assistant U.S. Attorney Joseph Dominguez said, "but they knew it would certainly make their cooperation all that much more stellar."

FBI agent Gregory Auld testified that since the Amish men's arrest, they had spoken at a dozen meetings attended by thousands of young Amish and Mennonites, where the pair warned about the dangers of drug use. "Those meetings were heart-wrenching," said Agent Auld. "It was genuine, and it had an effect."

These gatherings were so powerful, prosecutor Dominguez added, that he had even brought his family to one.

Judge Newcomer hadn't said much yet. He sat at his elevated platform, staring across the courtroom with a stern look on his face. It was time for the Abners to address the judge.

Before he spoke, Abner Two turned to the reporters sitting behind him in the spectator rows. He asked them to pass a message to young people everywhere. "Drugs won't do anything but take you down and get you killed," he said.

Then he stood and spoke directly to the judge.

"When I was a teenager, I got with the wrong crowd," he said. "Now I've changed my life around and gave my heart and soul to God. I apologize deep from the bottom of my heart."

For his part, Abner One broke down in tears as he tried to speak. He got out only a few words. "I lived a terrible life for a while," he said. "We want to try to do better."

Federal sentencing guidelines said the judge should send the Abners to prison for three to four years, but that was just a suggestion. Judge Newcomer had the authority to order more or less punishment.

The judge said he was impressed by all the glowing praise he had heard and by the evidence that both the Abners had begun to turn their lives around. He said he appreciated the way the young Amish cooperated after they were caught. But they did have to get caught first, he noted.

"These defendants," the judge said, "were responsible for bringing disrepute to themselves, their families and their community."

In the end, Judge Newcomer proved he was no newcomer to the bench. He spoke one way and sentenced another. He went lighter than the sentencing guidelines suggested, far lighter than most people in the courtroom expected him to.

Abner One and Abner Two each received one year in prison and six months of home confinement. And the prison time, the judge suggested, should be served on work release. If the Federal Bureau of Prisons agreed, neither of the Abners would be doing any hard time.

The prosecutors still sounded satisfied. "Part of the sentence for these two," Assistant U.S. Attorney Joseph Dominguez said, "is that for much of their lives, or at least for the foreseeable future, they'll be looking over their shoulders"—at monitors human and divine.

He didn't say that last part. But I'm pretty sure that's what he was getting at.

CHAPTER 13
THE BARBER OF BERGHOLZ

It was almost eleven o'clock at night, far too late for Amish neighbors to come calling, but there was a knock at Myron and Arlene Miller's back door. Five Amish men were asking for Myron, a bishop with the Mechanicstown Amish church in Carroll County, Ohio.

Though the visitors had awakened him, the bishop pulled himself together and tried to be polite. He opened the door and held out his hand to greet the visitors. Instead of stepping inside, they grabbed him, tugging at his long salt-and-pepper beard, which went halfway down his chest, and struggled to pull him outside.

"I saw the flash of scissors right by my head," recalled the forty-six-year-old bishop, holding up two fingers that he snipped together, mimicking the blades.

"They finally got him out on the cement out there and took a big pair of scissors and started to cut his beard," his wife said of the frightening home invasion.

The attack that night and others like it brought huge attention to the Amish of eastern Ohio. Much of it focused on a controversial sixty-six-year-old bishop named Samuel Mullet, who lived with his followers in an eight-hundred-acre settlement outside Bergholz, nine miles from the Millers' house.

This wasn't the first the Amish world had heard of Mullet. There'd been a lot of talk about the fiery bishop, especially about the kinds of punishments he liked to dole out. While many Amish bishops believed in shunning errant church members, few took it to the extraordinary lengths that Mullet did.

Almost anything could set the bishop off—from someone disregarding a minor church rule to someone else having the nerve to leave his church. Some ex-members alleged that he had forced men to sleep in chicken coops as punishment for ogling non-Amish women. There was even talk that he had coerced women to have sex with him to make them better wives. Mullet said it was counseling. His lawyer referred to him as the "Amish Dr. Ruth."

Amish bishops are generally reluctant to question one another's authority, but there'd been enough complaints about Sam Mullet that three hundred Amish bishops had gathered in Pennsylvania to discuss what they'd been hearing about him. After a long debate, they eventually decided to do what Amish bishops rarely do. They overruled one of their own. They reversed Mullet's shunnings. That infuriated him, leading some of his supporters to say that Mullet would certainly get his revenge.

Even in all their head-shaking over the colleague they had just overruled, none of the other bishops imagined that sharp blades would be involved.

Sam Mullet wasn't at the Millers' house the night of the scissors assault, but police said two of his sons and three other followers were, and Mullet was the man who had instructed them to go. He'd been especially annoyed, police said, that the Millers had helped his son Bill leave Mullet's Bergholz church several years earlier and that they'd also urged the young man to consider shunning his father.

In the father's view, if there was any shunning to be done in the Mullet family, it would be handed down—not up—the generations.

It was hard to say exactly how many beard attacks occurred. Samuel Mullet held a grudge against quite a few of his fellow Amish. The police said fifteen of Mullet's followers, at his request, had committed at least five attacks in four Ohio counties between September and November of 2011. But there were likely others too, perhaps quite a few of them—where the victims, in typical Amish fashion, didn't want to involve the outside authorities.

One reported attack occurred two hours before the visit to the Miller house. Police said the same group of men attacked Raymond Hershberger, a seventy-year-old Amish bishop in nearby Holmes County. The group got into Hershberger's house by saying they wanted to discuss religious matters. Once inside, they held the bishop down in a chair and used scissors and battery-operated clippers to shear off his long, white beard.

"We're here for Sam Mullet," one of the men reportedly stood and said.

In every one of these attacks, the authorities said, Mullet's supporters had shaved the beards or cut the hair of Amish people, including women, who had displeased him by questioning his authority, disobeying his rules or leaving the group.

Myron and Arlene Miller were well aware of the Amish tradition of solving conflicts through the church, but this was different.

"There's a lot of lives being messed up down there," Arlene said. "There's a lot of people being abused and brainwashed." It wasn't just that her husband had been assaulted. Other people were also at risk, including Mullet's followers. The Millers swallowed hard and called the police. They couldn't stomach the idea of others going through what they had.

Beards are not just facial hair for the Amish. Beards are a symbol of great importance and identity.

But first, forget mustaches. You'll never see an Amish man with a mustache. Like many things Amish, the reason goes back to the old days in Europe, in this case to generations of elaborately mustachioed German military men. When the Amish lived over there, it was military officers who wore mustaches. Since the Amish didn't serve in the military and hated being associated with anything military, they made a point of shaving their upper lips. Then Adolf Hitler came along with his little squared-off mustache. Many of the Amish were in America by then. Like most Americans, they loathed Hitler. As committed pacifists and often German Americans, it's possible they loathed him even more than most Americans did. As far as many Amish were concerned, the Führer ruined mustaches forever. To this day, virtually all Amish men, regardless of age, marital status, other facial-hair choice or unattractive upper lips, shave that little strip daily.

I have no problem with that. Personally, I think mustaches look kinda weird on anyone, Amish or otherwise. I've never had a mustache and never will, but beards are a different matter entirely, and not just because they indicate a man is married. To Amish men, beards mean maturity. They mean solid values and stability. They mean, "I am not vain. I'm not constantly rushing to a barbershop or making a fuss over my appearance. God gave me this beard, and I'm wearing it without apology."

For Amish men, growing a beard is right up there with Amish women not wearing jewelry of any kind or not cutting their hair and just wearing it in a bun. It's all part of not being showy.

Of course, there is plenty of hair talk in the Bible. "It is like the precious ointment upon the head, that ran down upon the beard, even Aaron's beard: that went down to the skirts of his garments." Look it up. It's Psalm 133:2. And for the ladies, in 1 Corinthians 11:15: "But if a woman have long hair, it is a glory to her." Just don't be showing it off!

The tiny town of Bergholz is about as remote as Ohio gets. Jammed into the northwest corner of Jefferson County, the land is hilly, and the people are spread widely apart.

Fred Abdallah, the Jefferson County sheriff, took a ride to Mullet's compound outside town to investigate the Millers' report. "He's saying that he didn't do it, but they consulted with him, they had a meeting with him," the sheriff told local reporters after he got back. "He knew who all the targets were going to be, he sanctioned it and he sure as hell never told them not to go."

Sheriff Abdallah said one of the other beard-cutting suspects mentioned something about the night of the Miller and Hershberger attacks: "If the clippers didn't break, we were going to get four more guys."

In nearby Holmes County, Sheriff Timothy Zimmerly was struck by something else: how rare it was for the Amish to turn to the civil authorities for help.

"We don't get many Amish coming forward willing to testify," he said, explaining the local bishops were giving the victims permission not only to provide law enforcement with written statements, but to actually testify in court.

It was enough to bring charges, the sheriff said—and to make them stick.

Sam Mullet was arrested. So were fifteen of his followers, including six women and the five men who had allegedly come to the Miller home. Three of those arrested were Mullet's sons. They all pled not guilty.

Before the trial began, the case was moved to federal court in Cleveland, allowing the prosecutors to charge Mullet and his followers with committing hate crimes. The prosecutors said the defendants had targeted hair and beards because of their special spiritual significance.

At the trial, no one denied that the beard attacks had occurred, though Mullet insisted he hadn't ordered them. The Millers testified, describing the night of the attack.

Raymond Hershberger's son Andy also took the stand. As the men held his father down, the son said, the older man "was shaking all over. He pleaded: 'Don't shear me. Don't shear me.'"

A child cried out: "Don't cut Grandpa's beard."

After the attacks, the son said, his aged father was so ashamed of his chopped-off beard that he stopped preaching and refused to go to a family wedding.

But the most emotional testimony of the trial came from the person who had known Sam Mullet the best: his own sister, Barbara Miller.

At first she had refused to even talk to officers from the Trumbull County sheriff's office, but the pain and fear eventually won out. She agreed to testify. She arrived in court in a long black dress and a white bonnet.

When asked to describe how her older brother had changed after he'd moved to Bergholz, she said: "He was more about violence, anger and hatred. More of the 'eye for an eye' syndrome. If he does it to me, I'll do it to him." It was almost like he'd shifted his loyalty from the New Testament to the Old.

The sister also said that her brother had become "angry, angry, very angry, screaming and yelling, and no one could do anything right, and you didn't know what set him off. He was a dictator."

In 2007, Barbara and her husband, Martin, and six of their seven children had gone to live in her brother's community. The couple quickly became uncomfortable with what they saw and left after just three months. "Everybody was like, I don't know, I can't say it . . . *zombies*," she testified. "There was no emotion."

Still, she said, she never could have imagined what happened four years later on September 6.

It was late, about ten thirty at night, when they heard a loud knock at the door. When she opened the door, outside, in the dark, she saw five of her sons, her daughter, and their spouses.

They came inside and went straight to Barbara and Martin's bedroom. There, the attackers pulled Martin out of bed by his beard. They grabbed Barbara, held her and forced her to watch as one of the men cut off her husband's beard with horse mane-cutting shears. One of the Millers' sons used battery-powered clippers to shave his father's head.

The terrifying violence wasn't over, Barbara testified.

Her daughter and daughters-in-law then used the same shears

to slice off two feet of her waist-length hair. Two of the women carried out the attack while holding infants in their arms.

As women in the courtroom wept, the Amish mother, who was related to fourteen of the defendants, said that she had wanted to hug one of her sons, but "they were not [her] boys that night."

Some of the sixteen defendants balked at the rules of the courtroom. They didn't want to put their hand on a Bible and swear to tell "the whole truth and nothing but the truth." Instead, they asked the judge that they be allowed simply to affirm the truthfulness of their testimony. The Amish, they said, do not believe in swearing oaths. In the end, none of the Amish defendants testified.

Lawyers for the accused argued that the case didn't belong in court at all. The beard cuttings were internal church discipline, they said—not a case of anti-Amish bias. "Why did they do this? I know it sounds strange—compassion," defense attorney Dean Carro told the jurors. "No crime has been committed. These were purely good intentions."

Other defense lawyers suggested that the beard and hair cutting were meant only to embarrass the men and women so they would reconsider their errant ways.

Mullet's attorney tried to portray his client as a well-meaning religious leader whose methods might be unconventional but were ultimately not a crime. The other church members knew what they were doing, he said. They weren't "zombies doing the bidding of Samuel Mullet."

Said Bryan: "This case represents a clash of civilizations, misunderstandings of a culture that most of us haven't spent time around, other than driving around Amish country and buying some fresh-baked pie and bread."

It wasn't clear—not at first—how much of this the jury was buying. But the prosecutor pressed ahead. These were crimes, pure and simple, Assistant U.S. Attorney Bridget Brennan said. And one man was behind them all. "Sam Mullet was the beginning and the end of all of these attacks," the federal prosecutor argued.

Jurors began their deliberations on a Thursday morning, September 13. They returned with a verdict one week later. The jury found all defendants guilty.

Samuel Mullet was convicted of federal hate crimes and of conspiracy for exhorting his followers to forcibly shear the hair and beards of those who opposed him.

Mullet's three sons, his daughter and eleven others including his nephews and niece were also convicted of hate crimes and conspiracy for participating in the attacks.

The sixty-six-year-old bishop faced life in prison for his crimes. U.S. District Court judge Dan Aaron Polster scheduled sentencing hearings for January 24.

The only question now was who would or wouldn't apologize and what their sentences would be.

Sam Mullet stood up and pleaded with the judge not to send him to jail. Despite the convictions, he still insisted, he hadn't done anything wrong.

Standing before the judge, his white beard reaching his chest, Mullet said the whole trial was unfair. "I'm being blamed for being a cult leader," the sixty-seven-year-old bishop said. "I'm an old man.

I'm not going to live a long time. I'm not going to be here much longer. My goal in life has always been to help the underdog."

If the judge was hell-bent on imposing punishment, Mullet said, he would like to serve the sentences of the others, who included four married couples. "Let these moms and dads go home to their families, raise their children, I'll take the punishment for everybody," he said.

There was actually a lot of altruism going on in the courtroom. One defendant, Lester Miller, asked the judge to spare his wife, Elizabeth, "to put her sentence on me," so she could look after their eleven children. Several defendants then asked the judge to give them all or part of Mullet's sentence.

But when Judge Polster began to speak, he didn't seem too swayed by all the defendants' pleadings. And he didn't sound ready to move off the court's usual "you did the crime, you do the time" approach.

This was a case of profound importance, the judge said. "Anyone who said this was just a hair- and beard-cutting case wasn't paying any attention."

The judge made clear he wasn't buying Mullet's attempts to minimize what had happened. These were serious and damaging assaults.

"The victims didn't suffer long-term physical injury," the judge said, but they were left with "emotions and scars for the rest of their lives."

He addressed all sixteen of the defendants.

"You did more than just terrifying them," he said of the victims. "You trampled on the Constitution, particularly the First Amendment." The Amish, if anyone, ought to know better than that, the judge said. "In my opinion, it was particularly reprehensible because each of you has benefited from the First Amendment to the Constitution," which guarantees freedom of religion.

"Each of you has received the benefits of the First Amendment, and yet you deprived your victims of the same," the judge said.

While some of the codefendants did apologize, the judge said he couldn't help but notice that Mullet never had. "I've concluded you deserve the harshest, longest sentence," the judge told him. "The attacks would not have occurred but for you. You ruled the Bergholz community with an iron fist. Your law was the law."

Sitting in the courtroom listening to the judge address her brother, Barbara Miller held a jacket to her face, hiding whatever emotion she felt.

And then the judge let loose.

He sent all sixteen of them to jail.

Mullet's fifteen followers, including the six women, all got more than a year in jail. The terms ranged from a year and a day to seven years, depending on exactly what roles they had played.

Judge Polster sentenced Mullet, who had turned sixty-seven, to fifteen years in federal prison for coordinating the bizarre beard-and-hair-cutting attacks. It was less than the life in prison prosecutors had asked for. But for a sixty-seven-year-old man, several people in the courtroom noted that fifteen years might be close to the same thing.

He was out of the realm of Amish forgiveness now. The federal courts are a far more punitive place.

CHAPTER 14
DON'T CLAPE ME, BRO!

They call it *claping*, though there's still some debate over where the word comes from.

The Amish have theories. Probably, the English people and the Mennonite people have theories, too. In Amish Country, everyone has theories about everything, whether the theories make any sense or not.

Some people say *claping* comes from the sound a stone makes when it hits the side of an Amish buggy.

Clape!

Maybe so. Others say it comes from the fact that when the English kids aren't hurling stones or rocks or chunks of construction debris at slow-moving Amish buggies or Amish people just walking down the road, sometimes they toss hard lumps of clay.

Those sting just as much. There's a lot of clay in Amish Country, and some of it really is hard as a rock.

To me though, the most likely explanation for the word is the meanest one: that it's a scrunched-together version of an ugly anti-Amish slur. The Amish are *clapes*. Clay apes. Farmers. Dumb people out in the sun digging in the dirt. So harassing them for fun—stoning an Amish buggy, blowing up an Amish mailbox, breaking Amish windows, trashing an Amish barn—falls under the cruel sport of claping.

What jerks!

When I was growing up in Lebanon County, it was the conservative Black Bumper Mennonites—so named because they are allowed to drive cars but only if they are painted entirely black, even the bumper—who were the worst. A lot of English people have trouble telling Black Bumper Mennonites from Amish, and I can understand why. They also speak Pennsylvania Dutch. Most dress plain, although if you look closely you can see some differences in style. Like the Amish, they are taught to be nonviolent.

That wasn't my experience of them, though. I remember being in a buggy and having a black car full of Mennonites cut in front of us and slam on the brakes. I don't know who was more startled, us or the horse. Once we were blocked from moving, they leaned out of the windows and pelted us with eggs.

This was happening all over the county. I couldn't understand why people who looked like us, sounded like us and mostly lived like us could be so mean and ignorant. I guess they thought they were better and cooler because they had cars. This was especially upsetting to the Amish adults because the adults in the two communities got along pretty well. But it got so bad that Amish preachers decided they needed to have a meeting with the Mennonite preachers. That didn't accomplish too much. The Mennonite leaders said they had no way of knowing which kids were responsible. Unless someone confessed, they couldn't do much about it. Of course, no one confessed.

Whatever muck claping bubbled out of, whether the clapers are English or Mennonite, clapings are almost always made up of the same four combustible ingredients: A carload of bored teenagers, usually though not always male. A quiet country road. Peals of stupid laughter. And little regard for consequence. A claping attack typically ends with the sound of squealing tires and the gnashing of Amish teeth, as the giddy clapers burn rubber out of there and their irritated targets wonder to themselves: "When will these dad-gum idiots finally leave us alone?"

In between, if everyone is lucky, no one gets badly hurt. Feelings and maybe a little property are the only things that get bruised. The clapers return to the back roads in boredom. The Amish return to their usual chores. The claping is chalked up to a uniquely Amish Country version of adolescent pranking, bothersome, no doubt, but fairly harmless most of the time.

But if you keep taunting people with firecrackers or rocks, eventually someone is going to get hurt. One dreadful night in eastern Indiana, a baby was killed.

Levi Schwartz, age twenty-seven, dressed in black pants, white shirt, black jacket and black, wide-brimmed hat, was at the reins of his lantern-lit buggy, driving his wife and six children home from a Tupperware party at his brother-in-law's house. This goes back a while to a humid Friday night in rural Adams County, Indiana, on August 31, 1979. About nine thirty, Levi and his family were heading north on Tile Mill Road outside the town of Berne when his wife, Rebecca, let out a piercing, "Ow!"

She was holding the baby, seven-month-old Adeline, and something hard—a chunk of tile, it turned out—smacked her left hand.

The wife hadn't seen anything, but her husband caught a quick glimpse of a red pickup truck speeding past them in the opposite direction with three or four people inside. He couldn't make out faces in the darkness, but he definitely saw the truck.

The baby didn't seem to notice anything. She hardly stirred at all. Maybe she stretched a little like she was coming out of a dream. Only when the Schwartzes got home and lit a kerosene lamp did the mother see the puddle of blood in little Adeline's ear. The child was dead by the time her husband ran to a neighbor's house, borrowed the telephone, called the county's central emergency switchboard and waited for the ambulance to arrive.

As is often the case with the Amish, the family didn't summon the sheriff about the baby's death. There was a single emergency dispatcher handling medical, fire, police, everything, so an Adams County sheriff's deputy arrived at the Schwartzes' house around ten thirty.

He asked what had happened. Levi provided a bare-bones account, including a basic description of the pickup. The deputy put that out on the radio. Shortly before eleven p.m., a deputy marshal in nearby Geneva stopped a vehicle matching the description, a red pickup. Inside were four young men, ages eighteen and nineteen, all recent high school graduates: Linn Burkhardt, Lynn Rich, Kevin Rehm and Thomas Wilkins. They had no criminal records. They hadn't been drinking or drugging that night. They all came from decent, local families. They had no firearms in the truck, though the deputies did find a fifty-pound nylon feed bag with thirty-three white rocks, ten ears of corn and ten pieces of red field tile, the square kind used in the main "field" area on a flooring job.

Before daybreak, all four had signed statements admitting they'd been cruising around the county in Burkhardt's pickup and at least a couple of them had thrown things at Amish houses and vehicles.

Or as one of the young men allegedly put it: "We decided to go out and get some clapes."

The investigators were sneaky or smart, depending on your perspective. They got the kids to admit the claping before any of them were told that a baby had been killed.

The following week, all four boys were charged with reckless homicide and released to their families on $10,000 bond. It wasn't that severe a charge, considering there was a death involved, and it started an immediate debate around town. Was this a freak, tragic accident or something darker? Everyone in Adams County seemed to have an opinion. By and large, most local people were pretty sympathetic to the defendants. "They're good boys," people said, "all from nice families." No one out-and-out condoned what they'd been doing, but almost everyone made a point of saying they unquestionably didn't intend to kill anyone.

The Amish certainly weren't out for blood. The families of some crime victims demand vengeance or the harshest possible punishment, but the Schwartzes were the opposite of that. They weren't demanding anything at all. Only reluctantly had Levi and Rebecca agreed to an autopsy. It found what everyone expected it to: Baby Adeline suffered a skull fracture and brain injury and died almost instantly. When asked about the frequency of local kids harassing the Amish, Levi allowed there was nothing new about that. It's "been going on for some time," he said. "They throw at buggies, windows, mailboxes . . . It's gone on for as long as I can remember."

As the investigators poked around, some disturbing details came out. Those local kids Levi said were harassing Amish families? It turned out that three of the four young men admitted they'd done this sort of thing previously, and the deadly attack on the Schwartz buggy was anything but spontaneous that night.

When questioned after his arrest, Kevin Rehm admitted vaguely that he had thrown things at the Amish "three or four times before." But written statements from three of his coworkers at Economy Printing added some ugly detail to that. He'd often come to work on Monday mornings, they said, bragging of his claping adventures from the weekend. He seemed especially proud of the night he'd hit an Amish kid with a corncob. There was blood all over the kid's face. Another time, he talked about tossing a wooden plank at an Amish while driving by at seventy miles an hour.

"Like some people went to a show every week, he went out and got Amish," one coworker said. Another said he'd warned Kevin someone might get hurt. Rehm supposedly answered: "So what? They're just clapes."

Thomas Wilkins told investigators in his confession that at about five that fateful afternoon, he finished his farm job and stopped by the service station where Lynn Rich worked. "He said something about, well, throwing stuff—claping is what he said. He asked if I wanted to go out with him." Wilkins, Rehm and Rich climbed into Burkhardt's red pickup, threw the feed bag in the back and hit the road. Before they ever came across the Schwartz family buggy, they'd torn a forty-five-mile swath across Adams County. They threw a rock at Jerry Girod's buggy, tearing a hole in the back. They pelted more rocks at Eli Weaver's buggy. They hit Andrew Hilty's house. Another rock busted a screen door and whacked Mary Shelter on the shoulder. She was sitting in her living room. As Jake Byler rode in his brother's buggy, something hit him on the hand. As well as the investigators could determine, the boys in the red pickup had hit four buggies, nine houses and an Amish school.

And why did they do all this? Tom Coolman, the Adams County sheriff, tried to probe that with Linn Burkhardt.

"What is the purpose of throwing objects at Amish?" the sheriff asked.

"I don't even know," Burkhardt said.

"For fun?"

"No, not really."

"You don't really have an answer for that question?"

"No, I don't."

The sheriff said later he thought 30 percent of local high school students had been claping at least once. Since the Amish so seldom report these incidents, the sheriff added, there wasn't much his people could do. "Some of the Amish had just stopped going out at night to avoid attacks," he said. "It makes it hard for us to enforce the law if they won't tell anyone what's happening."

A state police sergeant said Lynn Rich told him the whole thing was partly the county's fault. "He didn't want to sound like he was trying to make excuses," the sergeant said, "but if there were more things to do in Adams County, he and his friends wouldn't have to find their own entertainment."

Reporters swept into Adams County, giving the Amish another limelight they'd have much preferred to avoid. The story was all over national TV, how a prank gone bad in Amish Country had left a baby dead and an Indiana county facing tough questions. (Ultimately, a TV movie would even be made about the case. *A Stoning in Ful-*

ham County, based on the Schwartz case but with all the names changed, starred Ron Perlman, who went on to be a big deal in *Sons of Anarchy*, and a much-younger Brad Pitt as one of the youths in the pickup who felt torn over what he had done. "Religious beliefs clash with the law when an Amish infant is killed in a rural community!" the trailer said.)

The coverage sure made outsiders pay attention to the larger issue. It was the first time many people had ever heard the term *hate crime* used in connection with the Amish. Yes, harassing the Amish because they are Amish is a hate crime! For many non-Amish people, the death of baby Adeline and the arrest of those four boys was the first time that picking on the Amish was ever openly discussed at all. It was the kind of behavior that makes some Amish people want to turn the other cheek and makes others of us want to rise up in vigilante outrage.

In fact, there was nothing new about any of this. Amish people have been living with this for centuries. The claping back in Germany and Switzerland—persecution, it was called at the time—was far more severe. Not to downplay anything that's happened in America, but in those days, the Amish were martyred *on purpose*.

Various experts have been studying modern claping over the years. Credit professor Brian Byers and his colleagues at Ball State University for coming up with the first official definition. "Claping is a verb for predatory crimes perpetrated against the Amish by non-Amish persons, usually adolescents, rooted in anti-Amish biases." I'd say that's about right. They offered some subcategories, too. Along with claping, there is "dusting," speeding past an Amish buggy to irritate the occupants with a cloud of dust. There is "flouring," unleashing a bag of flour on Amish buggies while driving past, and vandalism directed at Amish property, such as blowing up mailboxes and turning over outhouses.

I can tell you all that stuff has happened where I live too, and the clapers can be fairly creative. One night in my early teen years, I was riding with my parents and several of my brothers and sisters when a group of Mennonite kids in a pickup truck attacked our buggy with giant globs of yogurt. Yes, yogurt. It did no real damage, but it made an awful mess. The bright white globs sure stood out against our flat black buggy. We needed brushes to scrub it off when we got home.

Byers did interviews with non-Amish people who admitted to claping. He was struck, he said, by the "group nature" of claping. One of his subjects said it would be "sick" to clape alone. Another person said: "It was a kind of male bonding . . . It kind of drew us all closer because we went out and did something."

Personally, I always thought claping was less of a problem in Lancaster and Lebanon counties than in some other parts of the Amish world. In the places where I've lived, there have always been lots of Amish around. The Amish and non-Amish work side by side, whether it's guys on construction sites or women and girls cleaning English peoples' homes. We volunteer together at the local food banks and fire companies. We bump into each other in the store aisles and even on the streets downtown. You can't say the two communities, Amish and non-Amish, are fully integrated—not even close, but we're not total strangers, either. That has to help.

Yet even in my area, claping has been a factor for decades. In his terrific book *The Amish in Court*, Wayne Fisher writes of one such incident in Lancaster County in August of 1960, long before I was even born. "Four youths were riding around near Leacock, Pennsylvania, when they passed several Amish women walking along the road. The youths stopped and turned around. One of them pulled a large stalk of corn from a nearby field and . . . two of the youths leaned out of the car and struck Mrs. Lydia L. Stoltzfus across the face with the root of the cornstalk. The strike broke her nose and shattered her glasses. When arrested and questioned about the incident, the youths said, 'We just don't like the Amish.'"

And it's never really died down.

A series of barn arsons lit up Lancaster County in 2001 and 2002, striking fear into the hearts of many local farmers, both Amish and non-Amish. It also reminded many of what had happened just ten years earlier in Mifflin County, Pennsylvania.

One frightening night in March of 1992, an arsonist drove around the Amish settlement of Big Valley. In just two hours, he (or they) set fire to seven barns, killing one hundred and seventy-seven horses and cows, causing more than a million dollars in damage. What fascinated the news people wasn't so much the scale of the destruction. Outside reporters were used to big tragedies. It was the way everyone, Amish and non-Amish, pitched in together to rebuild everything.

That was a spring of barn-raisings in Mifflin County. Nearly $700,000 was raised by the community and outsiders. The national reporters could barely believe their ears when they asked an Amish farmer if he wanted the arsonist caught and he replied with a shrug: "Only if he wants to do it again."

Asked what penalty might be appropriate, another man said he'd like to have him to dinner, show him how they lived and ask why he did this to them.

• • •

Lynn Rich and Kevin Rehm were the first to go on trial. The jury was assembled at the Adams County courthouse in downtown Decatur. Judge Herman Busse, who'd come in from Fort Wayne to handle the trial, took the bench. The courtroom was crowded with relatives and friends of the accused. No Amish were there.

Dan Sigler, the Adams County prosecutor, made his opening statement. He laid out what had happened on Tile Mill Road that night and gave a brief overview of all the evidence he had. It was a strong opening statement, everyone in the courtroom agreed. Then Sigler sat down, and it was time for the defense lawyers to speak. Instead, they asked the judge for a brief recess. The lawyers all went into a back room for a private conversation.

If the boys pleaded guilty, the defense lawyers asked Sigler, what kind of deal could they get? Would he reduce the charges? Would he recommend a lighter sentence? Would he say something nice about the boys to the judge?

No, no and no, Sigler said.

The best he could do, the prosecutor told the defense lawyers, was to make no recommendation about how long a sentence Judge Busse should impose. The boys' fate would be left entirely in the judge's hands.

It wasn't much, but the defense lawyers knew it offered one big benefit: The prosecutor wouldn't get to introduce all the evidence he had about all the claping Rich and Rehm had done—that night and earlier.

They had a deal.

The judge broke the news to the jurors. "You jurors don't have to divine this issue," he told them. "The monkey is now on my back."

He delayed the sentencing for a month, giving the county probation department time to write a pre-sentence report. It contained a lot of information that was favorable to the boys. It included letters from friends, employers—even their Sunday school teachers. It noted that the young men's families had reimbursed the Schwartzes for their medical and funeral expenses. It added that the dead baby's father, Levi, "held no malice."

There was even a letter from an Amish bishop saying that the kids had done wrong but adding:

"We believe that the four boys have suffered and suffered heavily since the crime, and they have more than paid for what they did." What the Amish community really wanted in this case, the bishop said, was "that it doesn't happen again."

Finally, sentencing day arrived. Under the charges the boys were facing, Indiana law said the judge could give them up to eight years in prison. Again, the courtroom was crowded with the boys' friends and relatives—and no Amish at all.

Judge Busse said he knew the Amish. They were good people. He said more people should be like the Amish. They don't believe in vengeance, he said. He said that in reaching a sentence, he was influenced by the spirit of the Amish.

Then he looked down from the bench at Rich and Rehm and their lawyers and handed the sentences down.

Five years in prison and $5,000 fines.

Then the judge suspended the prison term, meaning neither boy would have to spend a day in prison.

That wasn't the end of it, of course. In a way, these stories never end.

Soon after the first sentencing, the other two boys pleaded guilty as well. Linn Burkhardt, who'd been driving and didn't do any throwing that night, got three years' probation and a $3,000 fine. Thomas Wilkins, who'd provided prosecutors with the most information, admitted to criminal recklessness, a lesser charge, and got a two-year suspended sentence and a $2,000 fine.

A pretty sweet deal all around for people who'd killed a baby, wouldn't you say?

Levi talked to almost no one about how he felt about any of this. He did talk to one writer, Barry Siegel, who did an amazing piece about the case for *Rolling Stone* magazine. "A Quiet Killing in Adams County," it was called. A lot of people read that story.

"Sometimes I do feel angry," he said, "but I don't like having that feeling against anyone. It is no way to live."

He just wanted peace. That's all, he said. "If I saw the boys that did it, I would talk good to them. I wouldn't talk angry to them or want them to talk angry to me."

The punishment, the father noted, wasn't up to him or his family. He'd cooperated to some extent, he said. "I let them have an autopsy and gave them a long statement. I thought that was enough. I was just hoping it could be taken care of without me."

If he'd had to testify at a trial, he added, "[he] would just feel [he] had an enemy."

I guess I admire his forgiving nature, but when the hell are the Amish going to stick up for themselves?

CHAPTER 15
STITCHIN' WITH A B

There's a bishop who owns a hardware store just outside Intercourse. Bishop Gideon is his name. Late one October night, he was woken up by the sound of people banging around inside his store. The lights were off. It had to be burglars. But Bishop Gideon didn't burst in shouting. He didn't call the police. He didn't grab his hunting rifle. He waited quietly in the shadows until he got a clear idea of what exactly was going on.

He could see two men in dark English clothing. Their pickup truck was parked out back. The tailgate was already open, ready for whatever merchandise the men were able to haul out of the store. The first thing they grabbed was a pile of stepladders.

That's when the bishop slipped in behind them.

He too grabbed an armload of stepladders and carried them out to the truck.

"Let me help you gentlemen," Bishop Gideon told the startled burglars. "If you want these so badly, you can have them."

I think that scared the burglars more than calling the police ever would have. They glanced nervously at each other. They dropped the stepladders they were carrying. They jumped into their pickup truck. Tires squealing, they sped into the night, not even bothering to shut the open tailgate. Bishop Gideon just stood there, staring at the stepladders on the ground in front of him and watching the pickup's taillights disappear.

It was such a brief moment in time in a community where time has nearly stood still. One night at one store in one town in rural Pennsylvania. No one got famous. No one made a million dollars. No one got killed. The encounter had none of the elements that usually make a major story. The media never even showed up. Yet to me, what happened that night in Intercourse was profound.

"If someone slaps you on one cheek, turn to them the other," Luke 6:29 famously urges. "If someone takes your coat, do not withhold your shirt from them." That idea is at the heart and soul of Amish teaching, and the bishop really lived it that night. What a powerful concept! It's the kind of lesson that settles inside your head and plants little seeds in there. Who knows what might grow from that? Surely, it forces people to think.

I'm not certain how self-reflective those English burglars were. I'm guessing not very. But I'll tell you this much without fear of contradiction: They won't be returning to the bishop's hardware store any time soon.

I know lots of other stories like that one. True stories. Meaningful stories. Little stories with giant lessons. Stories profound in their own quiet ways. Amish life is packed with these grand gestures and little kindnesses delivered without expectation of payback. Houses rebuilt after devastating fires. Livestock rounded up after mass escapes. Meals carried to the sick and disabled before anyone even had time to ask. These are things that have happened to people I know personally, things that happened to me. My family remembers the outpouring after my father died. It isn't phony generosity, it isn't just for show. Many Amish people do this sort of thing even when no one's looking, and they don't brag about it next Sunday at church. Okay, sometimes they do, but not usually. A lot of Amish try to do what's right because that is what they believe in and it's what the church teaches them to do. It's right there in 2 Corinthians 9:7: "Each one must give as he has decided in his heart, not reluctantly or under compulsion, for God loves a cheerful giver."

Amen to that!

It's just too bad the Amish can also be so mean!

Yes, mean. Cruel. Harsh. Almost vicious sometimes. The Amish can be very judgmental and very unkind.

It's one of the genuine riddles of Amish society: how these very same God-fearing Amish men and women—these selfless barn raisers, these gracious burglary victims, these loving churchgoers tending to the sick—are so quick to trash their own neighbors, relatives and friends. There's no doubt about it: Those famous helping hands can become wagging fingers in a hurry. And that dual nature, which is almost never discussed in public, is one of the genuine unsolved mysteries of Amish life.

You think I'm exaggerating? Believe me, I'm not. It's just that most people never get to see this side of the Amish, because the Amish save most of this cruelty for their own friends and family.

Lying, cheating and scapegoating are far too common when the Amish do business with other Amish. Amish businesspeople are notorious for skimming the wages of people who work for them and treating their employees unfairly.

One Amish construction contractor I know stubbornly refuses to pay his workers on time even though he is plenty rich. "Let them complain!" he says with a shrug, confident that old-fashioned Amish passivity will shield him most of the time. Eventually, he gets around to paying—unless he conveniently "forgets."

Then he shows up for church on Sunday with holy devotion in his voice.

While I was younger, my brother Samuel and I went to work framing sheds for a man who owned a company near us. Our job was to frame each shed and shingle the roof. When we were done, the boss's nephew and another guy were supposed to apply the siding and the trim. Sam and I were clipping along at a nice, rapid pace. The other two guys were mostly goofing off, but the owner wouldn't blame his nephew for the backed-up production. He kept coming out and yelling at Samuel and me.

I was never good at holding my tongue, and this was seriously pissing me off. "Talk to your nephew," I tried to tell him. "He and his friend are the ones slowing everything down."

He wouldn't listen. Despite how obvious it was, he wouldn't believe the problem wasn't us. He just kept coming out and complaining loudly, in language not fit for Sunday dinner, until Samuel and I decided we'd had more than enough.

The following day, he started in again. "You and your brother are slow and worthless. I don't know why I'm paying you at all."

That was it. I picked up the staple gun I'd been using to attach the shingles. There must have been something in my eyes. When I looked over at Samuel, he seemed genuinely concerned. He should have been. I moved toward the boss with the staple gun in my right hand. He took a step back. I moved another couple of steps closer. He backed up again, stumbling on the gravel. That allowed me to gain on him.

I've never seen this guy or anyone else in his family move so fast. He righted himself and took off running toward his house. Believe me, Samuel and I didn't have to wait to get our final paychecks.

So much for Amish patience and honesty. The boss was quick with the blame and slow to see the problem caused by own blessed kin.

I don't know how long it took him to finish the shed without us. But it's like the Amish proverb says: If you are patient in one moment of anger, you will escape a hundred days of sorrow.

No one keeps statistics on the frequency of Amish harshness. If anyone did, you probably wouldn't believe them anyway. The Amish are just so loath to share their business with outsiders that neither the abused nor the abusers would tend to tell the truth. But I've seen it, and all Amish people have. The Amish may sound like polite, perfect little angels when the tourists pass through town, but when we're finally alone again, then it's finger-pointing time.

The Bible says speak kindly and thoughtfully and otherwise hold your tongue. This keeps coming up, especially in the New Testament. Ephesians 4:29: "Let no corrupting talk come out of your mouths, but only such as is good for building up, as fits the occasion, that it may give grace to those who hear." Proverbs 16:28: "A dis-

honest man spreads strife, and a whisperer separates close friends."
James 4:11: "Do not speak evil against one another, brothers. The
one who speaks against a brother or judges his brother, speaks evil
against the law and judges the law. But if you judge the law, you are
not a doer of the law but a judge."

And my favorite, Luke 6:31: "And as you wish that others would
do to you, do so to them."

Oh, really? Luke would have had a lot to say about Amish women
and their legendary quilting bees. That's where the trash talk begins,
innocently enough, with a roomful of Amish women sitting together
for the pleasure of one another's company and the purpose of making beautiful quilts.

Amish women love to quilt. They are patient and talented
quilters. There's no denying that. Their quilts win prizes at major
county fairs and high-class craft shows. Their products are bought
and collected by people around the world. As little Amish girls,
they sat for hours with their mothers and older sisters practic-
ing the intricate techniques. *Match, sew, match, sew, match, sew,
quilt. Match, sew, match, sew, match, sew, quilt.* They will keep on
quilting for the rest of their lives. From what I've heard from my
English friends, there aren't many skills that are universally passed
on like Amish quilting is. I've never known an Amish girl who can't
sew like a pro.

Any time an Amish girl is getting married, her mother sum-
mons a group of friends and female relatives to the family house.
She serves unsweetened black coffee and dry molasses cookies. The
women sit together and hand-sew for hours, creating lovely quilts
and comforters and anything else the newlyweds could possibly plop
on top of a mattress—besides themselves. Each quilt takes many,

many hours to finish. Quilting leaves lots of time to talk, and talk is what these Amish women do.

"Did you hear what Melvin's youngest did?"

"Did you hear what Hannah said to Abram?"

"Did you hear that Sarah's boy has a car now? He's driving on Sunday too!"

I call it a stitch-and-bitch party. The ladies are stitchin' and bitchin' all day long. One of my friends who's walked in on a few parties calls them sew-and-tell days. These quilting parties are one big gossip session, that's what they are. And there's never any chance the women will run out of comments about people's lives or fresh rumors to share.

"I heard Eli left the Amish . . . I heard the Millers have a new tractor that isn't allowed . . . I hear no one knows if Chester will ever have the nerve to show his face again in church. You heard what he did, right? There's no good way to seek forgiveness for doing *that*! Sleeping with a goat? Twice in the same night? After his wife warned him? I hear even the goat was disgusted!"

Ladies! Stop! Just stop!

All this stitchin' and bitchin' might sound harmless at first, just a few Amish women making quilts and sharing an ancient oral tradition. But from what I've seen, these "harmless" little get-togethers are the foundation of something much darker and more severe, the absolute, unbending refusal of the Amish to ever leave one another to their own business.

Truly, Amish women (and also men) will judge one another about *anything*. It could be something as hurtful as infidelity. Or it could be something as trivial as a hairstyle. A roomful of quilting women could just as easily devote an afternoon to either topic.

It's a shame no one's ever read the painted proverb plaque for sale at a local Amish store: "The person who sows seeds of kindness will have a perpetual harvest."

"Did you hear?" I walked into a stitch-and-bitch party at my mother's house to hear one of her friends exclaim. "Rebecca's boy got a haircut," meaning a *barbershop haircut*—without a bowl.

"That's so terrible," one of the other ladies said, commiserating. "I never thought he'd get a haircut. I feel just terrible for his mother. Unless she condoned it. You don't think she condoned it, do you?"

"Well, I certainly hope not!" the first woman huffed.

All that, over a silly haircut! And what next for that mother? The woman certainly risks a social shunning. Could the ladies really be seen socializing with someone who allowed her son to get a barbershop haircut?

I've heard it all. Someone else skipped church with no good reason, or drank too much, or got caught kissing a girl . . . who wasn't Amish . . . in the backseat of someone's car. With each new revelation, the knife sinks deeper. "His poor mother! I don't know how she'll ever live this down!"

The rumor is that Amish families don't have mirrors in their homes. Well, that's just not true. Mirrors are fine for shaving. They just need to be small, never full-length and never used to admire oneself or to take pride in personal appearance. But honestly, it wouldn't hurt for some of these gossips to look at themselves in a mirror before they prattle on about their neighbors' real or imagined faults! Mark my words: Next year will come around and the lady who's complaining this time will have a son who's done just what she's pointing fingers about now.

There truly is no end to this Amish busybodying. Trivial or important, half-true, might-be-true, someone-thought-they-heard-it, could-be-true-tomorrow—it's all fair game in the culture of constant commentary about other peoples' lives.

When I decided I wanted to get baptized in the New Order Amish Church, one of my older stepsisters was deeply offended. Lord only knows what she said behind my back, and she said plenty straight to me.

"That's not how you were raised," she yelled at me. "That's just not right. You go pray about this, you hear me? You're embarrassing the family."

"Thank you for your opinion," I told her as calmly as I was able.

Then I went and did what I thought was right for me.

And wouldn't you know it? Now her son has decided to get baptized in a New Order Amish Church! As far as I know, she hasn't said a single thing about it—certainly not to me!

I just bet the stitch-and-bitchers will have an opinion, though.

I think I understand where some of this comes from. Our faith is packed with rules and regulations, and daily living is an exercise in do-this-don't-do-that. The stakes could not be higher: heaven versus hell. And the inward-focused nature of Amish society creates a beehive effect in which we're all buzzing around each other twenty-four hours a day.

Living like that for so many generations has had its effects. One of them is clearly a lack of personal privacy and no real concept of "shut your mouth and mind your business." The Amish are famously meek and taciturn when visiting outside. Even the English burglars are treated with concern and respect. But heaven help the Amish community member who becomes the subject of unflattering gossip. I know, because I've been on the receiving end more than once. So has my family, and I promise you it isn't fun.

For reasons I've never been entirely sure of, people like picking on my family. Things that others seem to easily get away with become issues for our branch of the Peacheys and the Stoltzfuses: driving cars, drinking too much, dating the wrong people. Things that might well be overlooked in others become federal cases for us.

One reason, I'm convinced, is that the Amish are often uncomfortable with widows and widowers. It's almost considered a failure if one spouse dies young. In our family, that happened twice—with my dad and with my stepfather's first wife. But that's not the only reason we're so often under the microscope (and the binoculars, too). The special scrutiny we've faced could also be due to the vibrant personalities we have. I'm not shy or retiring. Certainly, none of my brothers are, and my stepbrothers aren't introverted, either. We're loud. We're considered rambunctious. Some of us have gotten into minor scrapes and trouble with neighbors and even the law. There's no denying we're all filled with energy and spirit. We do stand out. In some communities, that might be looked on as a plus, but standing out is rarely a good thing in Amish Country.

You can just imagine how some of my Amish friends have reacted to the *Amish Mafia* TV show and all the attention it's generated. Let's just say the controversy and publicity aren't universally appreciated.

I've been attacked by strangers and critics, not to mention every two-bit politician from Harrisburg to Washington and back, for things I have said and done on the show. Just wait 'til they read this book! But I don't know them, and frankly, I don't care so much what they say. It's a little different when people I've known forever start attacking me for things I am tremendously proud of. I have thick skin—I have to, but still, that's no fun.

I understand that partly, it's the Amish quest for privacy. I realize I've exposed some long-simmering secrets, though nothing that would personally hurt anyone I care about. I've told some truths that very much needed telling, but there's also a heavy dose of jealousy in here. I'm sure of it. Along with the praise I've gotten, I know there are lots of people talking behind my back right now. I've just come to expect that, and these aren't just my mother's quilting friends. These are people of my generation too, including kids I grew up with, guys I know from my Rumspringa gang or from just out running around. From time to time, one of them will approach me directly.

"Oh, you think you're somebody now," an old friend said one day. He definitely sounded angry. "Who do you think you are showing the Amish to the world?"

This wasn't an overly sensitive TV critic. This was a guy I'd known since I was a kid. "Actually, no," I answered. "I'm pretty much the same as I've ever been. Just Levi."

That wasn't the first time someone talked to me like that, and I've come to expect it sometimes, depending on the crowd. But the first time it happened I was genuinely surprised.

"You shouldn't be talking about these things on television," said an old drinking buddy, a guy I've known from hanging out in sports bars and playing softball. "You're working against the church."

I was caught off guard and decided to rib him a little. "How do you even know about the show?" I asked him. "You've been watching television?"

Okay, that was a cheap shot, but I couldn't resist it. This friend might have been watching the Phillies on the sports bar's big-screen, but that didn't explain how he knew about Merlin or Alvin or Ruck Davey.

It's always funny hearing Amish complaints about something the traditional Amish aren't even supposed to see. "I heard about it," is often the answer.

But television-watching habits aside, I didn't like the accusatory tone of his comment. "How's telling the truth working against the church?" I asked my old friend. "That's just telling the truth."

"It's a bad reflection, you showing off like that on television," he said persistently.

His words didn't strike me as fair or warranted. He didn't know what was inside my head and he wasn't exactly living his life above reproach. *People in glass houses . . .* , as the saying goes.

I decided it was time to give a little back. "You go to bars dressed Amish," I told him. "Aren't you showing yourself off? That's disrespecting the Amish right there."

"Oh," he said, "are you judging me?"

"No," I told him. "But it sounds like you're judging me."

I could feel it coming. Our talk was slipping into stupid fast. I was ready to end it, but my friend was not.

"You're judging me," he repeated.

I was wrong, he maintained, for using my place on a television program to bust some myths. But, just like it says in John 8:32, I knew I wasn't doing anything wrong: "And you will know the truth, and the truth will set you free."

I just shrugged and said: "At least I'm not pretending I'm something that I'm not."

I knew he'd be gossiping about me tomorrow.

CHAPTER 16
VALENTINE'S DAY IN COURT

There's a big rumor that the Amish don't pay taxes. The rumor isn't true. I'm not sure what your tour guide told you, and I don't care what you heard from someone at the molasses-cookie shop. The Amish pay income taxes, property taxes, sales taxes, federal taxes, state taxes, inheritance taxes, capital-gains taxes, so many taxes it's impossible keep them all straight. And we complain about those taxes just like most Americans do. We hate 'em and we pay 'em, year after year.

It's right there in the Bible, Mark 12:17: "Jesus said to them: 'Render to Caesar the things that are Caesar's, and to God the things that are God's.'" The Amish do plenty of rendering to God, and I don't have to tell you how many Caesars keep coming around with their hands out, the United States Internal Revenue Service being only the most famous and most despised.

The Amish could never get away with not paying taxes. We ride on public roadways, we walk on public sidewalks, we drink water from public reservoirs, we benefit from the protections of the United States military, even though we don't choose to sign up. Those things aren't cheap, and someone has to pay for all that. Not paying taxes would make us freeloaders, and that is something we are not.

The Amish pay taxes, all except for one.

We don't pay Social Security taxes.

That doesn't mean we don't have Social Security numbers or Social Security cards or even a file down at the Social Security Administration. I have all those, like almost all Amish do, whether they work on or off the farm. When so many don't have driver's licenses, that's our basic ID card. It's something you need to open a bank account or get a hunting or fishing license. Don't forget, many Amish people won't carry photo identification of any sort, and plenty don't vote. That Social Security card becomes important, even if they never make a single contribution to the federal retirement program or accept a single penny of benefits.

Therein lies a fascinating piece of Amish history that reveals a lot about the relationship between the Amish and the outside world.

The story features a crotchety Amish farmer named Valentine Byler, who had a long red beard and lived in New Wilmington in western Pennsylvania. He's dead now, but for more than half a century, old Valentine has been a quiet inspiration to tax haters everywhere. Recently, his name was even whispered in the fight over Obamacare. We'll get to Valentine in a moment, but just know that while most Americans have no choice about paying their Social Security taxes, Valentine considered it his moral, Amish duty not to pay his.

This all goes back to 1935, when Congress passed the Social Security Act. That law required most Americans to pay a small percentage of their wages into a retirement trust fund. When those people reached retirement, checks would start arriving in the mail. Social Security was a key part of President Roosevelt's New Deal, pulling America out of the Great Depression and lifting millions of older people out of dire poverty. It's one of the most popular and successful government programs ever devised. If you don't believe me, try running for office just about anywhere but an Amish community and promising you'll kill Social Security. Good luck with that.

It took twenty years, but in 1955, Social Security was extended to people who worked on farms, and that's when the Amish started to care about it.

The Amish hated the whole idea of Social Security.

It's the family's job and church's job, they believed—not the government's—to care for people when they get old or sick. A group of Amish bishops laid out the principle clearly, as soon as they realized that Social Security could soon apply to many Amish: "It has been our Christian concern from the birth of our church group to supply those of our group who have a need, financial or otherwise." The whole idea of insurance payments and benefit schemes, they said, was really ungodly.

Pennsylvania farmer Valentine Byler agreed with the bishops. He was totally anti–Social Security. He said his religion forbade him from buying any kind of insurance, the private or the government kind. Told that Social Security wasn't exactly insurance, the farmer supposedly waved a small-print government document, stroked his red beard and fumed: "Doesn't the title say 'Old Age, Survivors and Disability Insurance'?"

It sure did.

Valentine was far from alone in not wanting Washington's Social Security. In 1959, fourteen thousand Amish people, more than one-third of the entire United States Amish population at the time, signed a petition asking Congress for a special religious exemption from the whole program. "We do not want to be burdensome," they said, "but we do not want to lose our birthright to everlasting glory, therefore we must do all we can to live our faith!"

The IRS really wasn't in the everlasting-glory business. This was a tax-collection agency. The two sides made some effort to negotiate. Meetings were held between the Amish bishops and IRS supervisors, but talk of a compromise got nowhere. The IRS finally decided enough time had passed, and it was time for the Amish to pay up!

"We don't ask people their race or religion when we administer the tax laws," the chief of collections in the IRS Pittsburgh office pointed out. Therefore, "people have no right to use their religion as an excuse not to pay taxes."

The dispute was starting to sound like one of those old you-must-pay-the-rent movie-house melodramas featuring a mustachioed villain and a damsel in distress.

"You must pay the Social Security tax!"

"We won't pay the Social Security tax!"

"You must pay the Social Security tax!"

Neither side sounded ready to budge. Valentine Byler was the issue's Amish poster boy—although, since he was Amish, he couldn't have his picture on any posters, of course.

The IRS took the case to court, filing a lawsuit in 1960 against him and several other Amish defendants at the U.S. District Court in Pittsburgh. Valentine was summoned to appear, but he didn't show. He was cited for contempt. The U.S. Marshals drove out to New Wilmington and found Valentine at his farm. They put him in their car and drove him back to the courthouse in Pittsburgh. When the Amish farmer finally stood before the bench, the judge didn't seem angry with him. It was the government agents he reamed out.

"Don't you have anything better to do than to take a peaceful man off his farm and drag him into court?" the judge demanded before dismissing the government lawsuit outright.

The agents didn't miss a beat. Valentine still had an unpaid Social Security tax bill, and it totaled $308.96, going back four years. The IRS finally moved to collect.

On April 16, 1961, while Valentine was out plowing the fields for his annual spring planting, IRS agents came to his farm. The agents seized three horses and some harnesses and sold them at auction to satisfy the bill.

Agency officials explained themselves in a lengthy press release: "Since Mr. Byler had no bank account against which to levy for the tax due, it was decided as a last desperate measure to resort to sei- zure and sale of personal property. It was then determined that Mr. Byler had a total of six horses, so it was decided to seize three in order to satisfy the tax indebtedness. The three horses were sold May 1, 1961, at public auction for $460. Of this amount, $308.96 represented the tax due and $113.15 represented the expenses of the auction sale, including feed for the horses, leaving a surplus of $37.89 which was returned to the taxpayer."

Keep the change, Valentine!

To get his plowing done, he borrowed a horse from a neighbor.

IRS officials said later they got no pleasure from seizing and auctioning Valentine's horses, but what choice did they have? "The Byler case, like all others in the same category, presents an unpleas- ant and difficult task for the Internal Revenue Service," the agency said almost apologetically. "We have no other choice under the law."

The agents did seem to be on solid legal footing, but there was something they failed to anticipate: the public-relations fiasco their horse seizure would cause. The national media went berserk. The *New York Herald Tribune* complained: "What kind of 'welfare' is it that takes a farmer's horses away at spring plowing time in order to dragoon a whole community into a 'benefit' scheme it neither needs nor wants, and which offends its deeply held religious scruples?" The Norfolk *Ledger-Star* called the seizure "a milestone in the passing of freedom—the freedom of people to live their lives undisturbed by their government so long as they lived disturbing no others. It was a freedom the country once thought important."

The rhetoric got a little overheated at times. One Amish man told *Reader's Digest*: "Allowing our members to shift their interdependence on each other to dependence upon any outside source would inevitably lead to the breakup of our order."

There is only so much bad press any government bureaucracy can withstand. The IRS officials didn't back down immediately—not yet—but some of the fight seemed to drain out of them.

A meeting was called in Washington in September of 1961. The Amish bishops sat down with Mortimer Caplin, commissioner of the IRS. This time, the bishops didn't argue the law. They began by citing Bible verses—and not the one about Caesar. This time, they started with Timothy 5:8: "But if any provide not for his own, and especially for those of his own house, he hath denied the faith and is worse than an infidel."

It all seemed cut-and-dried to the Amish, but Timothy didn't seem to sway the men in suits and ties, nor did any of the other scripture the Amish bishops quoted. Nor did the new petition the bishops left with Commissioner Caplin and his people that day. "We believe in a supreme being and also the constitution of the USA, and we feel the Social Security Act and Old Age Survivors Insurance is abridging and infringing to our religious freedom," this one said. "We believe in giving alms in the church according to Christ's teaching."

With all the Bible quotes and references to Christ's teachings, the meeting seemed more like a church service than a legal debate. "Our faith has always been sufficient to meet the needs as they come about," the new petition went on, "and we feel the present OASI is an infringement on our responsibilities; as a church we feel grieved that this OASI has come upon us."

The meeting didn't have the sweeping results the Amish had hoped for. Caplin didn't exempt the Amish, but they got something for all their trouble. The IRS commissioner issued a moratorium on seizing horses for payment.

That victory wasn't nearly enough for Valentine Byler. He was ready to file a lawsuit, which was a huge leap for an Amish man, a major breach of Amish tradition. The Amish do not like going into court under any circumstances, much less to launch a highly contentious battle with the United States government. But a lawyer was hired, and legal papers were drawn up, as Byler felt like he had no choice.

As the court date grew near, the bishops pleaded with him not to go forward with the suit. This wasn't the Amish way, the bishops argued—any more than paying Social Security taxes was. Valentine knew in his heart that the bishops had a point. At Valentine Byler's request, in January 1963, U.S. District Court judge Rabe Marsh signed a stipulation dismissing the case.

The bishops assured Valentine Byler that they hadn't abandoned him or the important cause he had championed, they just had another approach in mind. Instead of a lawsuit, they said, they would seek relief from Congress and the president, the same two branches of government that had created Social Security in the first place.

It worked.

In 1965, the House of Representatives passed the Medicare bill, expanding the Social Security safety net to provide medical care to millions of older Americans. Buried in the bill's 138 pages was a brief provision exempting the Amish and similar religious groups. That was the door they needed to crack open. A special rider was added and soon the exemption was expanded to cover regular Social Security, too.

The Senate approved the bill in July, and the law was signed by President Lyndon Johnson on August 13, 1965. That made it official, and the Social Security Administration canceled the tax bills of fifteen thousand Amish.

It was a great victory for Amish tradition. It would leave older Amish men and women completely dependent on their families and the church to care for them in later life, and it would add a whole new load of pressure on the bishops and other elders to make sure that really happened in the years to come.

Bishop David Fisher didn't sound worried about that.

"We take care of our own people," he said, "and if we start paying in, the next generation will collect, and we don't want government handouts."

There was happiness across Amish Country. The great power and majesty of the federal government had bowed to a small but passionate church.

Sadly, one person was not able to share fully in the Amish celebration. Valentine Byler never got to toast the victory that his objections had helped to spark. On May 3, three months before President

Johnson signed the Amish exemption to Social Security and Medicare, Valentine was on his farm in New Wilmington when he fell from a grain drill and broke his neck.

It was a terrible accident, and it left him nearly paralyzed. He could barely use any part of his body. He really couldn't speak. His recuperation, if it ever came, was going to take months or years.

When August came and with it the news from Washington, Valentine was lying quietly in a hospital bed in the front room of his farmhouse, which was the cheeriest room in his house.

Told what had just happened, he seemed to understand, though no one could really say for sure. One witness reported the slightest flicker of a smile crossed Valentine's lips, framed by his long red beard.

CHAPTER 17
SCHOOLED IN FORGIVENESS

It was the bloodiest day ever for the Amish in America. It also produced the greatest Amish lesson ever taught, and it all unfolded a ten-minute buggy ride from my family's Lancaster County farm.

On Monday, October 2, 2007, Charles Carl Roberts IV walked into a one-room schoolhouse in the Old Order Amish community of West Nickel Mines. He arrived just before 10 a.m. There were twenty-six children at the school that day, plus the twenty-year-old female teacher Emma Mae Zook, her twenty-two-year-old pregnant sister-in-law Lydia, her mother Barbie, and three more visiting moms with infants.

A thirty-two-year-old milk-truck driver, Charlie was well liked in our part of the county. He wasn't Amish, but he had lived and worked around the Amish for most of his life. His father was a retired police officer. He had a wife named Marie and three sweet young children, ages two to seven. He was constantly doting on them. He had finished his milk route that morning, making pickups at a couple of dozen Amish dairy farms. He'd grabbed a quick nap at home, walked his older son and daughter to their school bus, hugged the children good-bye, stopped at a hardware store to buy some flex ties and driven his pickup truck to the West Nickel Mines School. As usual, the front double doors were open. The Amish aren't big on locks.

Charlie arrived with a secret. What no one else knew was that for nearly a week he had been stockpiling quite an arsenal: a Browning twelve-gauge shotgun, a Ruger 30-06 bolt-action rifle, a Springfield XD nine-millimeter semiautomatic handgun, six hundred rounds of ammo, several cans of black powder, an illegal stun gun, some construction lumber, a hammer, a screwdriver, bags of nails and screws, K-Y Jelly and an empty five-gallon bucket.

Once inside the school, Charlie pulled out his handgun, abruptly stopping Emma Mae's German lesson. He ordered the boys, who were dressed in their usual Amish dark pants and suspenders, to help him unload the truck. The boys did as they were told, while the gunman began sealing the building's entrances with his lumber. He shoved a heavy foosball table toward the front double doors, but not before the teacher and her mother managed to escape.

Charlie was agitated. Things weren't going as planned. He sent one of the boys outside to find the teacher and bring her back.

Charlie had a plan. He told the fourteen boys to leave. Next he told the four remaining adults, "You ladies can leave. Those with children."

A nine-year-old girl, who spoke only Pennsylvania Dutch, didn't understand Roberts's English when he demanded: "Stay here. Do not move. You will be shot." She innocently followed her brother outside.

That left a total of ten girls still in the schoolhouse. It was the girls he was interested in.

Charlie didn't say anything the girls could make sense of. But he did rant a bit. "I'm angry at God and I need to punish some Christian girls to get even with him," he said. "I'm going to make you pay for my daughter."

The girls quietly huddled together, looking frightened in their long dresses, bonnets and plain shoes, not knowing that the whole outside world was about to fly into panic.

The teacher and her mother had already run to the farm of a non-Amish neighbor, Amos Smoker, and asked him to call 911. "There's a guy in the school with a gun," Smoker told the dispatcher at 10:35 a.m.

As the state police sped toward the school, Charlie bound the girls' feet and ordered them onto the floor. Then he told them to get up again and stand in front of the chalkboard.

Hanging above their heads was a prominent sign that people would notice later. It was bordered by yellow-and-black smiley-face stickers and read: "Visitors Brighten Peoples' Days."

"Be quiet," he snapped at the girls.

By then, police were roaring up White Oak Road with sirens wailing and were converging on the tiny schoolhouse. They didn't want to rush the building for fear of what the gunman might to do to his hostages. They didn't want to wait, fearing exactly the same thing. A trooper called out to him over the PA system of his cruiser, telling Charlie to toss his weapons out and let the girls go. They got no answer. Using his wife's cell phone, Charlie did call 911, telling the dispatcher: "I just took, uh, ten girls hostage and I want everybody off the property or, or else."

He didn't sound angry. He didn't yell or scream. Lancaster County district attorney Don Totaro said Charlie's voice sounded "flat . . . It's almost like there's no soul there."

By then, a large and growing crowd had gathered outside—neighbors, parents, police, paramedics, a farmer with two large dogs.

Inside the school, the girls could see that Roberts was growing even more agitated. He was pacing and barking orders and mumbling to himself. Something was about to happen. That was obvious. Several of the older girls had a powerful suspicion about what that might be.

"Shoot me first," said Marian Fisher, thirteen, the oldest one.

"Shoot me second," said her eleven-year-old sister, Barbara.

And Charlie did.

One by one by one, starting at 11:07 a.m., he shot all ten of the girls at point-blank range, beginning with Marian Fisher and her sister and not skipping anyone. He fired more than two dozen rounds in all. He did it quickly and efficiently. Then he pulled the trigger one more time, shooting himself in the head.

"Mass casualty on White Oak Road," one of the responding troopers shouted over the police radio at 11:10 a.m. as others tried frantically to force their way past Roberts's heavy barricades. "Multiple children shot."

The carnage was heavy. Marian Fisher and Naomi Rose Ebersol, seven, died instantly. Anna May Stoltzfus, twelve, was dead on arrival at Lancaster General Hospital. Lena Zook Miller, eight, and her sister, Mary Liz, seven, died the next day in their mother's arms. Five girls, including Marian's sister Barbara, were wounded but survived. Several of them, the doctors would say later, were saved because they had buried their heads in their arms.

When the troopers finally burst inside, the murder scene was a bloody, chaotic mess. Even some veteran law-enforcement agents had trouble absorbing it all. The crime-scene investigators kept walking outside to regain their composure and take a few breaths of fresh air.

"We had all these victims at the scene that we're triaging," state police commissioner Jeffrey Miller said later. "We didn't know who they were. We just knew we had a young, female victim that was taken to hospital X." The nurses had to take digital photos of the victims' faces and e-mail them to the state police, who showed the photos to the teacher so the girls could be identified.

Word spread quickly across the fields and along the dirt roads of Amish Country. The Amish turned out. From all directions, men and women walked to the West Nickel Mines schoolhouse. They stood outside. They covered their faces, and they wept.

The Amish weren't the only ones to suffer that day. For the stunned family of Charles Roberts, the loss and the shame were almost unbearable.

"I heard the sirens and heard helicopters," his mother, Terri Roberts, said later. "My phone was ringing and it was my husband, and he said, 'You have to get to Charlie's right away.'" She heard the first radio reports in the car: a shooting at the West Nickel Mines School, not far from where she knew her son delivered milk. Her mind raced with possibilities. What if her son had been shot trying to rescue the children?

She pulled into Charlie's driveway. Her husband was standing with what looked to her like sunken, swollen eyes.

"Is Charlie alive?" she asked.

"No."

Losing an innocent child is excruciatingly painful. Losing a guilty one isn't one bit easier. Terri Roberts's initial reaction was that she and her family should immediately move out of town.

In the hours after the shooting, relatives of the young Amish victims began showing up at the killer's mother's door. Not in anger, but in love, and every one of them had the same message for her.

Do not leave. Forgiveness is genuine. We are all in this together.

"Is there anything in this life we shouldn't forgive?" one of the Amish women asked.

Terri Roberts wasn't quite sure how to answer. She could hardly believe her ears.

These peoples' young daughters had just been shot and murdered. Her grown son—or some evil spirit that inhabited his mind and body—was responsible for that. Were the Amish really this understanding? Was their famous forgiveness really that strong? Could it overcome even mass murder?

Maybe so.

The police and media were already asking the usual "why" questions. Why did this happen? Why did Charles Roberts snap? What would provoke a man who'd never exhibited violent tendencies to act so abhorrently? These were the most innocent of victims. These were children whose families he'd known.

His grandmother Teresa Neustadter spoke with the cluelessness that all Charlie's relatives felt. "What is there to say?" she asked. "He was a good grandson."

Nothing made any sense at all, though Charlie might have planted some clues in the four suicide notes he left for his wife and children. He said he had molested two female relatives twenty years earlier, which would have made him twelve at the time. (When they were asked about this, the now-grown women said nothing like that had ever happened to them.) In one of the notes, he said he had been having dreams for the past couple of years about doing again what he did twenty years ago.

If he was worried about harming little girls again, why do something even more terrible to them?

In one of the notes, he mentioned the death of his own first daughter, Elise, who been born prematurely and lived just twenty minutes. That actually did occur.

But how did any of that explain a massacre? Was there something in the comment he made in the final minutes about his "need to punish some Christian girls"?

It all sounded like crazy talk, and the grieving Amish relatives really didn't seem to care. They were moving forward. Their focus, they said, came right out of the Bible. To them, the Word of God seemed perfectly clear.

Hadn't Jesus admonished in Matthew 5:44: "Love your enemies and pray for those who persecute you"? Hadn't Paul taught much the same thing in Romans 12:18–21? "Live peaceably with all. Beloved, never avenge yourselves but leave it to the wrath of God . . . No, if your enemy is hungry, feed him."

It's true that many religions give lip service to the idea of forgiveness. Forgiveness and reconciliation are deeply embedded in the Christian, Jewish, Islamic and Buddhist faiths—and lots of others, too.

But how many people would do what these Amish families did—do it so quickly, so fully and with so little reservation or regret?

Immediately forgive the children's killer and reach out with love and support to his devastated family? Not many, that's for sure.

Soon after the shooting, Charlie's wife, Marie, was at her parents' house when she saw a group of Amish men approaching. She was nervous but her father said, "You can stay inside, I'll go out and talk with them." What she saw next she says she will never forget.

The Amish men hugged her father.

Terri Roberts was surprised when dozens of her Amish neighbors attended her son's solemn funeral. They followed as he was buried in an unmarked grave in his wife's family's plot behind Georgetown United Methodist Church.

"There are not words to describe how that made us feel that day," she said. "For the mother and father who had lost not just one but two daughters at the hand of our son, to come up and be the first ones to greet us—wow!"

She was surprised again when the grieving Amish relatives invited her and her daughter-in-law to attend the girls' funerals.

They went, of course.

Eleven days after the shooting, the old schoolhouse was torn down. It was too painful for people to look at. Some Amish parents also felt their children would never be comfortable attending classes in a world-famous crime scene. Since Charles Roberts had taken his own life and wouldn't be standing trial, there was no need to preserve any forensic evidence. A volunteer crew of Amish carpenters, alongside some of the grieving fathers, made quick work of the old school.

A new schoolhouse would have been easy to build for a people who can raise a barn in a single day. But the pain was fresh and no one seemed in any hurry to build anything. Students returned, but for nearly six months their lessons were taught in a garage.

In the spring, a new school was finally constructed a few hundred yards away. This one was called the New Hope Amish School. By the time teachers and scholars (the Amish word for students) stepped into the new one-room school, most of the media had packed up their notebooks and microphones and driven their satellite trucks home—or, more likely, on to the next big human tragedy. Few in the Amish community were sad to see them go.

CHAPTER 18
GIRLS GONE

The Amish sisters were twelve and seven years old. The girls, Fannie and Delila, were keeping an eye on their family's roadside farm stand while their parents and brothers and sister were up at the barn milking cows. There were fourteen Miller kids in all. Dusk was settling gently on upstate New York.

Then a white sedan pulled to a stop.

There was nothing unusual about any of this. The girls often helped around the stand, waiting on customers and arranging the displays of vegetables, fruits, jams and other products from the family farm. But in the car, authorities said, were Stephen Howells Jr., age thirty-nine, and his twenty-five-year-old girlfriend Nicole Vaisey—and *normal* isn't the word anyone would use for them. The car windows were open, and the girls noticed a dog.

"You want to pet the puppy?" the man allegedly asked. "His name is Kaleidoscope."

The girls did love dogs. This one, a golden retriever–Doberman mix, was leashed in the backseat on the driver's side. So the girls leaned in the open window to get a better look.

Something seemed off to Fannie. She didn't know exactly what, but she motioned to her little sister as if to say, "Let's get out of here." It was then, the authorities believe, that Stephen Howell reached around from the front seat and yanked both girls into the car, stepping on the gas and speeding away.

In many ways, the Amish make perfect targets.

They live in isolated communities, ride around in slow-moving vehicles, and they walk great distances, often alone. Though their lives are mostly insular, they do rely on outsiders for help. "May I use your telephone?" "Do you know what time it is?" "Can I rent some space in your garage?" Amish children play together for hours with little adult supervision. Physical security is the last thing on Amish peoples' minds, and when something bad occurs, the Amish are famously slow to alert outside authorities, preferring to settle as much as they can strictly among themselves.

The good news in this case is that the girls' parents, Mose and Barbara Miller, realized quickly that their daughters were gone and promptly walked to a neighbor's house, where they telephoned the police. The police activated the New York State AMBER Alert, announcing that two girls had vanished around 7:20 p.m. on August 13, 2014, from their family farm stand on State Highway 812 at Mount Alone Road in the small Amish farming community of Heuvelton, twenty miles from the border with Canada.

"Fannie Miller is about 12 years old with brown hair and brown eyes," the alert read. "She is approximately 5-feet tall and weighs about 90 pounds. She was last seen wearing a dark blue dress with a blue apron and black bonnet. The victim is also cross-eyed. Delila

Miller is about 6 years old with brown hair and brown eyes. She is approximately 4-feet tall and weighs about 50 pounds. She was last seen wearing a dark blue dress with a blue apron and black bonnet. She has a round scar on her forehead and is missing front teeth."

The AMBER Alert generated worldwide publicity, and the media descended quickly on upstate New York. In a matter of hours, hundreds of civilians had volunteered to help search. Crime victims, everyone agreed, don't get much more sympathetic than these two. But still, the hunt got off to a rockier start than it should have. There were no photographs of the girls.

When the state police asked the Miller family for photos of the missing girls, the parents said they didn't have any. The Amish, as the police should have known, don't believe in being photographed.

"What about a sketch artist?" one of the lead investigators suggested.

Frantic as the girls' parents were, even that seemed to cause them some distress. The parents weren't sure about the Amish teaching on realistic drawings. Did those carry the same vanity risk as photographs?

The police found a sketch artist who could speak Pennsylvania Dutch and did the best they could. The Millers finally agreed to release a sketch of the older daughter—but not the younger one, and valuable hours were lost.

By the time the volunteers fanned out across St. Lawrence County and the media satellite trucks arrived from Boston, New York, Syracuse and Montreal, Stephen Howells and Nicole Vaisey had already driven the girls to their home in Hermon.

Neither Howells nor Vaisey had a criminal record. They both had respectable-sounding jobs—he as a registered nurse in a wound-treatment center at Claxton-Hepburn Medical Center in nearby Ogdensburg, she as a professional dog groomer. But this was one creepy duo, if the stories police and prosecutors would later piece together are even halfway true. St. Lawrence County district attorney Mary Rain called the couple "sexual predators."

Once they got the girls back to their house, the sisters were "handcuffed together at the ankles and handcuffed to the bedpost because they were scared they were going to go out the window and flee," said Detective Sergeant Brooks Bigwarfe.

According to Bigwarfe, Howells and Nicole Vaisey had been on the lookout for little girls to grab. "She called it a shopping trip," said the sergeant. "They wanted to make the two girls their slaves."

And the kidnappers weren't planning to stop with these two, District Attorney Rain said. "There is no doubt in my mind that if they were successful, they were going to continue with future acts," the prosecutor said.

"There was the definite potential that there was going to be other victims from these two," St. Lawrence County sheriff Kevin Wells agreed. "They were looking for other opportunities to victimize." According to the sheriff, Howells and Vaisey weren't targeting the Amish in particular. They were simply seeking "opportunities."

By the time the girls had been held for nearly twenty-four hours, the story of the kidnapping in Amish Country had exploded everywhere. The AMBER Alert and the hard-charging media had done their jobs—and then some.

The kidnapping was front-page news in the *Watertown Daily Times* and *Daily Courier-Observer*. The *New York Times*, the *Bos-*

ton Globe and the Montreal *Gazette* all flew people in. The story was saturating the radio and the TV news—and not just on the local channels. CNN and Fox couldn't seem to get enough. The Millers didn't have television on their farm in Heuvelton. But Howells and Vaisey certainly did at their house in Hermon. The story was creating an uproar and attention that no one could possibly have bargained for.

It seems the kidnappers got spooked.

"They decided to drop the kids off in an isolated area," reported Sergeant Bigwarfe from the sheriff's office. Vaisey went first, scouting the area around County Route 20 in nearby Richville to make sure no police or civilian searchers were lurking around. When she reported all was clear, Howells drove Fannie and Delila to a dark spot in the road and shoved the two frightened girls out of the car.

As quickly as he'd grabbed them, he let them go.

It was dark outside. The girls didn't see any houses at first, but after walking for a couple of minutes, they came up to one. The lights were on. They rang the bell, not knowing who or what they might find.

An English couple answered the door. Their names were Jeffrey and Pamela Stinson. They were understandably startled by what they saw.

Two wet and cold little girls in Amish dresses, perfectly well mannered, with fear just dripping out of their eyes. The younger one didn't say much.

"Do you know where 812 is?" the older girl asked Jeff Stinson. "Can you take us to 812?"

"Yes, of course," his wife answered for him. "We know where that is."

Like everyone in St. Lawrence County, the Stinsons had heard about the missing Amish girls. They understood immediately that these had to be the girls on the news. The wife told the girls to come inside.

Her husband asked if they were hungry. They said they were. He cut up a watermelon he'd just pulled out of the garden. The girls devoured it in less than a minute.

"Can you take us home?" the older girl asked Jeff Stinson. "We want our mom and dad."

"We sure can," he said.

And so he did. He didn't think twice about what might happen if someone saw a grown English man riding at night across St. Lawrence County with two Amish girls. He piled the girls into his truck and began the fifteen-mile drive home.

"We never gave any thought about the implications or dangers," he said later. "We knew they had to get home."

As they rode along through the darkness, Stinson couldn't help but notice that a car seemed to be following them. He could only imagine who might be driving. He wondered if the truck was about to be shot at. He ticked off the miles in his head. The mystery car stuck with them until just before they reached the Millers' home. Then it sped away.

Two days later, the police arrested Stephen Howells and Nicole Vaisey. Each of them was charged with two counts of first-degree kidnapping and assault, crimes that carry a possible twenty-five years to life in prison. Both defendants pleaded not guilty. District Attorney Rain said more charges were likely on the way.

Outside a preliminary court hearing at the St. Lawrence County government building in Canton, Nicole Vaisey's lawyer, Bradford Riendeau, worked hard to portray his client as another of Howell's helpless victims. She was a woman desperate for attention, he said, with a boyfriend who liked sadomasochistic sex. "She was in a master-slave relationship," the lawyer said. "She appears to have been the slave, and he was the master. She's not as culpable as he is."

The lawyer mentioned something about homemade sex tapes.

"You've heard of *Fifty Shades of Grey*?" he asked a local TV reporter. "This was the fifty-first shade of grey."

The following week, after the girls had a chance to get settled at home, Jeff and Pam Stinson took an evening drive to Heuvelton. The whole Miller family warmly welcomed them inside.

Fannie and Delila were doing about as well as could be expected, said their mother, Barbara Miller. "We feel relieved we have them," she said, adding almost apologetically, "It's still not like it was."

The girls hadn't spoken much about the ordeal, said one of their twelve siblings, a nineteen-year-old sister, Mattie. "It just makes it scarier for them."

Citing his Amish views on forgiveness, the girls' father, Mose Miller, said he wasn't angry at the couple who had kidnapped them. He felt sympathy, he said. "It's sad," he explained. "They must have ruined their whole life."

There were a lot of thank-yous and handshakes on State Route 812 that night. The Stinsons left with a big bundle of flowers and a large bag of fresh vegetables.

But that friendly visit between English and Amish, family to family, rescuers and victims, isn't where this story ends. As the criminal case inched its way forward through the St. Lawrence court system, the Miller family of Heuvelton seemed to feel they should do something more for the Stinsons of Richville.

As the Stinsons saw it, they hadn't done anything extraordinary. They had simply acted as any decent people would. Two cold and hungry sisters had rung their doorbell one night. They invited the girls in. "We just brought the children back to their parents like they needed to be, as soon as possible," Pam Stinson said.

"If those are my children," her husband added, "that's what I hope somebody would do for us. If they were our daughters—we have girls—somebody would have brought them back to us."

But the Millers wanted to do something. Finally, they came up with an idea.

The Amish are famous for their barn raisings, where the whole community turns out to help a neighbor who has suffered a fire or some other calamity. But Jeffrey and Pamela Stinson didn't need a new barn. They had, however, recently lost a garage while they were away on vacation in Maine. As best as anyone could figure, a stray cat had knocked over a battery jump-start box. Their garage went up in flames.

To the members of the Miller family, that could mean only one thing: a garage raising at the Stinsons' place.

"They won't take no for an answer," Jeff Stinson told his wife, Pam. What choice did the Stinsons have?

They said "sure" and "thank you" and watched in awe as a big mob of Millers and friends, dressed in traditional Amish garb, descended on the Stinson yard like an army of fire ants and built a spacious new garage at greased-lightning speed.

But what about the other house, the one in Hermon where How-ells and Vaisey lived before they were taken off to jail? The house where they'd shackled the two young girls and held them against their will? That house was a chilling reminder to everyone nearby. It was creepy, the neighbors agreed, just glancing that way.

"You can't help but look over there," said next-door neighbor Jamie Matthews. That modest country home was suddenly looking like a diabolical House of Horrors. "You just shake your head in dis-belief," Matthews said.

The house was getting famous, Matthews noticed. "We've wit-nessed hundreds and hundreds of cars that drive by at twenty-five, thirty miles an hour," he said. "You know what they're doing. They're looking at the property. They're curious."

The people who lived nearby said they really didn't know this couple who'd been all over the papers and the TV news. "They kept to themselves," said neighbor George White. "They weren't out and about. It was a shock. We just don't understand."

The neighbors all agreed they ought to do something, they just didn't know what. Then Jamie Matthews heard the Amish kidnap-ping House of Horrors was for sale. A light went off in his head. He would buy that house, and then he would tear it down.

"It's important," he said, "not only for us but for the community to change the looks of that property."

He didn't hesitate another minute. He called the Realtor and offered the asking price, already planning the demolition in his mind.

CHAPTER 19
BAD BREEDING

The state dog warden paid a visit, and he did not sound pleased.

Orlando Aguirre didn't cite Elmer Zimmerman for animal cruelty, but the stone-faced warden did give the Amish dog breeder seventy-two hours to get thirty-nine of his poodles, shih tzus and cocker spaniels to a vet. The dogs, which were packed in tight wire cages on Elmer's corn-and-cattle farm, needed urgent treatment for flea and fly bites, the inspector said. Otherwise, the fines could go to $300 per dog.

Like many Amish farmers in Pennsylvania Dutch Country, Elmer Zimmerman had started breeding dogs on the side. He specialized in fluffy lap pups. You'd be amazed how much money city people will pay for those yappy little dogs. Dog breeding must have seemed like a natural choice to Elmer. He had the land on Kutztown Road in Berks County and plenty of room to throw up some wire-cage kennels. Like many Amish farmers, he could certainly use the extra cash, and didn't he already know a lot about raising livestock? How different could dogs really be? Pound for pound, it turned out, dog breeding was far more lucrative than raising cattle or horses.

The puppies (and their mommies and daddies) certainly had smaller appetites.

Elmer called his company E & A Kennels, the E for Elmer, the A for his wife, Arlene. The operation was tiny compared to some of the mega dog farms that were popping up nearby, especially in Lancaster County, but his business had grown to be sizable. He had seventy dogs in his kennels when the state inspector showed up that late-July day.

Elmer wasn't home at the time to see Inspector Aguirre come and go. But Arlene was, and she was frantic when Elmer got back around 5:30 p.m. She was gripping a blue form the dog warden had left, citing multiple kennel violations. Elmer had a phone he used for the business, and he called the number on the paper, but the warden had already left for the day. Around 8 p.m., Elmer phoned Dr. Frank Moll, a local veterinarian who had treated his cattle before, but not his dogs.

"He believed that he had to get immediate treatment for the dogs," the vet later told a local reporter, Ron Devlin of the *Reading Eagle*. "He was adamant that the dog wardens were going to return the next morning to see if he complied with their order." But getting the dogs treated by a licensed veterinarian could be expensive, so Elmer told the vet he had another plan.

He would shoot them.

Dr. Moll told Elmer there wasn't anything illegal about shooting animals in Pennsylvania, including dogs. "I warned him, though," the vet added, "that it was not the preferred method of disposing of dogs. I told him the Humane Society probably wasn't going to like it."

But Elmer pressed ahead. He used a twenty-two-caliber rifle. He had to reload many times. He started shooting and he didn't stop until he'd finished off all the dogs. Not just the thirty-nine the dog warden had cited, but all seventy of the animals in his kennel. Then Elmer's brother, Ammon, who had a breeding operation on his farm next door, also got into the act. He shot and killed ten of his dogs even though his kennel hadn't been inspected when Elmer's was. Together, they buried the bodies in a compost heap nearby.

There weren't any outside witnesses to the slaughter, so no one besides Elmer and his brother knew the precise details: how they were assembled for the shooting, what order the dogs were killed in, how long it took and what kind of fight if any the doomed animals put up. Did they bark or whimper? Did they try to run away? Did they seem to understand what was happening? Did the later ones watch the earlier ones get killed?

But there couldn't be much doubt about the basics. That next week, state dog wardens came back to Kutztown Road and unearthed the physical evidence. Just as Elmer had reported, eighty dogs in all took bullets to the head.

The Zimmerman brothers were far from alone in the commercial puppy-making business. Experts estimate there are now five thousand high-volume dog breeders in the United States. The vast majority of animals sold in pet stores and on the Internet come from these so-called puppy mills. Some are licensed operations, some are under-the-radar mom-and-pops, others might as well be called torture chambers.

Some of the facilities are downright medieval. I know because I've been inside a few of them. Puppy-mill dogs live a miserable existence. Instead of walking on grass, the dogs spend their lifetimes

on painful wire flooring in cramped rabbit hutches. The open flooring makes the cages easier to clean. Instead of collars or bandanas,
the animals wear livestock clips on their ears. They eat whatever's
left over at the farm. Frequently, the dogs aren't even given names.
The puppies are shipped off as soon as possible, sometimes literally
yanked from their mothers' breasts. The females are often forced to
breed twice a year. After seven or eight years of service, the breeding
females are often starved to death or led into a dark cornfield and
shot. What good are they at that point? They can't breed anymore.

Millions of puppies come out of these cruel mills every year,
just as millions of dogs are put to death at the nation's animal shelters. Those two figures are hard to separate. With so many new puppies being born, there just aren't enough good homes to go around.
Taken all together, the experts say, the mills are a huge part of the
reason for the overpopulation and dangerous inbreeding of American canines.

So what are the Amish doing in the middle of something so
shady? There's no doubt that they are. According to one recent
count, there were 277 licensed dog breeders in Lancaster County
alone and probably two or three times that many of the unlicensed
kind. I'll bet two-thirds of both categories are owned by Amish or
Mennonites. If you doubt me, take a drive against the background
of rural Pennsylvania or Ohio or Indiana or New York and look
for a crude hand-lettered sign: PUPPIES FOR SALE. Those roadside
signs are supposed to convince you that a well-loved family dog
just had a litter. More likely, somewhere out back is a large-scale
puppy mill you definitely won't be invited to tour. The famously
gentle people aren't so gentle with their dogs. I'm a lifelong dog
lover, so it breaks my heart. I'd hate to think of anyone treating

my beloved Cookie like that. She's the sweetest dog ever and way smarter than I.

Cookie is a poodle. She's a small dog and doesn't shed too much. She lives in the house with me. I hate hearing about people who force their dogs to stay in a cage while they're at work or sleeping. I don't mean just the uncaring breeders, I mean people with family dogs. They say they love their pets, then lock them up like prisoners. It's cruel, and I can't imagine being that mean to an animal.

When I was young, my family always had a dog on the farm. Lady, a beautiful brown German shepherd, was a part of our family for ten years. She was our greatest protector. We never had to lock our doors. Like a lot of other families we knew did with their own dogs, my father would take Lady once a year to an Amish breeder in Lancaster. When the litter was born, we'd sell the puppies. One year, the breeder wrote my father a letter. "I'm sorry to tell you that your dog has died." We never learned exactly what had happened, but everyone in our family was sad. We really loved that dog. When she'd left to go to the breeder, she was a happy, friendly, healthy dog, but something obviously happened.

Back then, we didn't know much about puppy mills, but we had our suspicions that Lady wasn't taken care of right. I don't think anyone knew what was going on with some of those breeders.

More people do know now, and some of the conditions have improved as a result, I believe.

Despite the bursts of public outrage and occasional media attention, the bad ones never get stamped out for good—for the same reason they have always survived. They make money, and the well-intentioned laws are never enough. Outsiders complain about animal overpopulation, and the American Kennel Club purists wring their hands, but raising dogs in large numbers can be a very profitable business, if you aren't too squeamish about the messy details.

How do Amish puppy breeders justify all this to themselves and to the outside world? They do it the usual way: by pointing to the Bible. It's right there, they say, in the very first book of the Old Testament. Genesis 1:28 says: "Then God said, 'Let us make man in our image, after our likeness. And let them have dominion over the fish of the sea and over the birds of the heavens and over the livestock and over all the earth and over every creeping thing that creeps on the earth.'"

Dogs aren't people. They are animals. We have dominion over them.

Or as one Amish farmer put it a little more vividly when the question of animal cruelty first popped up: "We country people do not look at dogs that much different from other animals. When you have livestock, you have deadstock. Why is this such a big issue?"

The Amish didn't invent puppy mills. Credit (or blame) for that goes to Midwestern farmers who started breeding dogs during the Great Depression to help make ends meet. Over the decades, the idea spread east. So many Amish farmers have now branched into commercial dog breeding that some animal-welfare activists now call Pennsylvania Dutch Country the "puppy mill capital of the United States."

Just don't expect to see this slogan on the license plates any time soon. You certainly won't find any mention of puppy mills in the Amish tourist literature. If you ask the people at the tourist bureau, you'll get a wall of blank stares. The idea of dogs spending their whole lives in narrow cages, never allowed outside, rarely taken to the vet, forced to breed relentlessly, then killed when they get too old or too sick to sell or procreate—that's not exactly the image the tourist-promotion people are going for.

Puppy mills really began exploding in Amish Country in the late 1970s and early 1980s. The animal-rights group Pet Watch New Jersey cites a crucial meeting of Midwestern farmers in November of 1981: "Several hundred Amish and Mennonite farmers were told they could raise and sell puppies to the public and pet stores alike, and with little or no overhead, they could make a fortune. Centrally located, Lancaster County was easy pickings for customers in Maryland, Delaware, New York, New Jersey and New England."

Animal welfare groups have been sounding a warning about these Amish puppy mills ever since. They "treat puppies as a cash crop," said Wayne Pacelle, president of the Humane Society of the United States. "I don't like to pick out a particular group," said Thomas Bougher of the Pennsylvania Dog Law Enforcement Office, "but the Amish are a significant part of the problem. Most people treat dogs as quasi-human, but a dog is the same thing as a chicken to them."

Main Line Animal Rescue, which has saved thousands of Amish Country dogs, offers several commonsense tips to dog lovers who want to avoid getting cage dogs from puppy mills. Don't patronize breeders who ship dogs to customers or sell too many breeds at once, the group suggests. That is common sense, but another of the warning signs, number three, might come as a surprise to some people— or maybe not: "Beware of ads in newspapers with phone numbers starting with 717 area codes"—the number for the Harrisburg-Lancaster-York area of south-central Pennsylvania. "Some of the

most infamous puppy mills in the country can be found in Pennsylvania's Dutch Country."

Public outrage about the Zimmerman case did not quickly die
down. Many things were said about the Amish farmers' decision to
shoot the dogs, but one thing wasn't said—that shooting those animals was a violation of the law. "It's horrible, but it's legal," admitted
Jessie Smith, special deputy secretary of the Pennsylvania dog-law
bureau. He, like most non-Amish, sounded appalled. "That someone
would shoot seventy dogs rather than spend money to do a vet check
is extremely problematic," he said, but there wasn't much, it seemed,
the state could do unless the laws of Pennsylvania were changed.

So on a Friday night, three weeks after the dogs were murdered, more than a hundred people gathered on Kutztown Road
at the end of Elmer Zimmerman's farm. Partly, they came to rally
for a law change. Partly, they came to hold a vigil for Elmer and
Ammon's dead dogs. As the people arrived, Elmer parked a tractor
at the entrance to his farm, blocking the crowd from coming onto his
property. So that is where the people stayed.

The moon was full. The protesters lit candles. They sang "Amazing Grace" and said some prayers. They placed eighty chrysanthe-
mums and eight dog biscuits next to Elmer's tractor. Several people
from pro-animal groups delivered highly emotional eulogies.

"These were dogs with no names," said Jenny Stephens of North
Penn Puppy Mill Watch. "These were dogs that none of us ever
knew. These were dogs who never knew the kindness a human hand
can offer and these were dogs who died a violent and terror-filled
death with no one to comfort them."

A lot of people got teary-eyed at that.

Howard Nelson, CEO of the Pennsylvania Society for the Prevention of Cruelty to Animals, said he'd cut short his vacation and driven straight to Kutztown Road. "It's not uncommon for puppy millers to shoot or drown their dogs instead of spending money on medical care," he said. "There may have been some spite in this case, but I'm just calling it pure evil. Every humane society in the state would have taken those dogs."

Harry Brown of the Main Line Animal Rescue seconded that point. "We would have taken them and not filed charges," he agreed. "That way, the animals survive and the kennel is out of business, a win-win situation."

As the vigil rolled on, the talk got more political. Speakers called out the names of "guilty" legislators who hadn't endorsed efforts to tighten Pennsylvania's dog laws. Interestingly, the list included several from the Lancaster area. One was State Representative Dave Hickernell. Another was State Representative Gordon Denlinger, who had just been defending dog breeding as "an issue of farmland preservation" and said, "There's a certain question about the removal of a person's livelihood. Should an animal enforcement officer be able to throw a person out of their occupation on a given day?"

Comments like that didn't make him any friends at the rally that night.

After the shooting, Elmer Zimmerman had done the best he could to defend himself and other Amish dog breeders. He told Ron Devlin of *Reading Eagle*, who covered the story, that he really didn't think he had much choice when he decided to kill the dogs. Things were busy at home that night. He had fifty cows that needed milking, and his wife was frantic. He said he didn't realize he could have taken the animals to a local shelter, as the animal-rights people were saying now.

"A lot of them were old, and I doubt they could have been adopted," he said. "We decided the best thing to do was to get rid of the dogs. I thought there was no other way."

But the animal-rights people weren't close to done. They were already thinking beyond the Zimmermans. They vowed to continue until the laws of Pennsylvania were changed, making heartless puppy mills illegal once and for all. It wasn't like the Zimmermans were the only dog breeders who had kept their animals in metal cages. They certainly weren't the largest. Probably, they weren't even the worst.

New cases kept popping up, and the activists turned their attention to the Pennsylvania legislature. They focused on something called House Bill 2525. It promised sweeping changes to the state laws governing breeder dogs and their puppies. The proposal would have banned wire floors, prohibited cage stacking, required annual vet checks, doubled the minimum floor space for dog kennels and given all dogs access to outdoor exercise areas. It would have given people like dog warden Orlando Aguirre a whole new set of enforcement tools.

Sensing public outrage, quite a few state politicians jumped on board.

"The decision by commercial breeders to kill healthy dogs instead of paying to repair a kennel and seek veterinary care is alarming and will likely outrage many people," State Secretary of Agriculture Dennis Wolff said. "Until our state's outdated dog law is changed, kennel owners may continue to kill their dogs for any reason they see fit, even if it is simply to save money."

Ed Rendell, who was then the governor, had followed the Zimmerman case closely. He said he was committed to ending Pennsylvania's reign as the puppy-mill capital. He even held his own noon rally on the state capitol steps in Harrisburg, declaring his support for the puppy-mill law.

"There are a lot of special-interest groups in this building fighting to defeat this legislation," Governor Rendell said. "What does it say about us that we allow people to shoot and kill dogs?"

The governor introduced Maggie, a small retriever he'd adopted from Main Line Animal Rescue after she was rescued from a Lancaster County puppy mill. Rendell said Maggie's ticket to freedom was that her third litter was stillborn, making her unprofitable to the kennel operator. He said she's small for her breed because she lived in a rabbit hutch for two years before being rescued.

"You can see she's very happy now," he told the crowd. "At this point, Maggie wakes up every morning and says, 'Thank God I'm not pregnant.'"

The delicate issue of Amish tourism was raised. Jana Kohl, an animal activist from Chicago whose grandfather started the Kohl's department-store chain, said she'd like to see dozens of puppy-mill billboards near the major Amish-tourism sites.

"Two thousand of the country's ten thousand commercial breeding kennels are owned by Amish and Mennonites," Kohl said. Dog lovers across the country, she said, should "shame and embarrass them by putting as many billboards and ads in as many places as possible. We can point the finger to Pennsylvania as aiding and abetting this horrific business that is nothing more than legalized torture."

A campaign like that could do damage to Amish Country tourism, Kohl seemed to be warning Pennsylvania officials. "A lot of people with a lot of money and resources are prepared to venture into a campaign like this," she said. "It's going to be a bigger and more embarrassing campaign than people expect, and it's going to shock."

Apparently, the Amish tourism officials heard that message loud and clear.

Janet Wall, vice president of Pennsylvania Dutch Convention & Visitors Bureau, showed up at Ed Rendell's capital rally to express her group's support for the puppy-mill reforms of House Bill 2525. "Abusive breeders should be put out of business immediately and permanently," she said in no uncertain terms. "Our voices must rise up as one."

But in the end, what the reformers got was a big disappointment. As House Bill 2525 worked its way through dark corridors of the legislature in Harrisburg, small changes were made. Then medium-sized changes. Then some bigger ones. Before the dog lovers knew what had hit them, the sweeping reform they were hoping for felt more like crumbs.

The new rules did ban dog shooting, and that was a good thing. They called for larger cages and regular vet visits. But many of the smaller puppy mills were exempted from the tighter rules. The law applied to only 650 of the state's 2,750 licensed kennels. And much of the enforcement was put in the hands of the industry-friendly Canine Health Board.

Governor Rendell tried to sound upbeat when he signed the puppy-mill bill into law.

"The advocates and ordinary dog owners and dog lovers made their voice clear," he said in a special signing ceremony in the

Bucks County vacation community of Langhorne. "You guys did this."

But with all the limits, waivers and exceptions in the new rules, no one expected puppy mills to disappear in Pennsylvania, and they didn't. In fact, one of the most notorious puppy-mill owners from Lancaster County, Daniel Esh, reeling from all kinds of well-deserved bad attention, tried to outwit buyers and inspectors by changing his kennel's name. It went from being Clearview to Scarlet Maple.

He and his father, John Esh, had a long list of black marks against their names. In 1996, they were accused of selling a rabid golden retriever named Toby to a family in Pittsburgh. The dog bit a child, resulting in the first and only case of dog rabies in recent Pennsylvania history.

The following year, the Eshes were accused of selling hundreds of sick dogs. A state inspection of their unlicensed kennel found Yorkies, poodles, spaniels, shih tzus, Rottweilers and Jack Russells with eye infections and rotting teeth. The animals were covered in feces. The Pennsylvania attorney general filed a lawsuit.

These humans acted worse than animals. Their dogs lived in sweltering heat in summer and frigid temperatures in winter. Larger-breed dogs were made to live in cramped cages with broken wire. Smaller-breed dogs didn't even have that much. They were kept outside with no shelter or bedding at all.

The name change didn't work. Daniel had his state license revoked again in 2009. His father decided the strict new state regulations were too tough for him. He closed the barn doors on his Scarlet Maple kennel for good.

Or at least that's what he said he was doing.

But in 2013 John Esh was caught advertising a company called Green Mountain Toy Puppies online. He had to pay a $175 fine. That wasn't even one-half the cost of one of the puppies he was selling. His son Daniel, the one who'd once sold a dog with rabies, was also in court. He pleaded guilty to having unlicensed dogs without rabies vaccinations.

For people like the Eshes, this is all just a cost of doing business, a very small cost for a very lucrative business. No one really expects the Amish to be out of the puppy business any time soon.

CHAPTER 20
THAT'S RICH

There's an old Amish proverb: "If you want to feel wealthy, count the blessings that money can't buy."

And that's certainly one way to do it. Another way to feel wealthy is to own a large working farm in Pennsylvania or Ohio at a time when land values are flying through the roof. A lot of Amish families have done that. Or you can get in early on America's organic-produce craze and be a key supplier to large supermarket chains. That's another one that turns out well for some Amish. Or you can take an English-driven bus down to a nice house on the gulf coast of Florida and spend the winter there riding bicycles and playing shuffleboard while your brethren up north shiver with woodstoves and no electricity.

Hey, why suffer through the cold?

Clearly, some Amish people these days are counting the blessings that money *can* buy.

Abundance comes in two flavors, the preachers like to say— spiritual abundance and material abundance. The truly fortunate get to experience both.

Just ask Moses Smucker. Moses started out selling handcrafted leather goods from a leaky tobacco shed in Churchtown, Pennsylvania. His Smucker's Harness Shop was quickly pulling in millions of dollars a year outfitting the Budweiser Clydesdales, the Ringling Bros. and Barnum & Bailey circus horses and the pampered pets of Saudi princes and country-music stars. Customers still wait six weeks and pay up to $50,000 for finely stitched harnesses that take eight pairs of hands to make.

Or ask Sam Mullet, the imprisoned Amish bishop convicted of sending his followers to cut the beards and hair of believers who had displeased him. When the fiery bishop was arrested, he had more than $2 million from oil and gas leases on his eight-hundred-acre farm in Bergholz, Ohio, prosecutors said. They wondered why Sam needed the government's help paying his legal bills. Hadn't his wife just offered to pay off one child's mortgage with $60,000 in cash?

Or go ahead and ask any of the well-off Amish farmers in Holmes County, Ohio, who've earned up to $6,000 an acre from oil and gas companies eager for fracking rights to the land. Environmentalists hate the idea. Some of the neighbors have been cheated by lease hounds who know how much the Amish hate to sue, but many Amish landowners have hit fracking bonanzas over the past few years. They're the Holmes Hillbillies, liquid gold gushing beneath the feet of these famously plain people.

God must have put the natural gas down there for a reason!

Whatever you do, do not pity "the poor Amish."

As a group, the Amish aren't poor at all. Quite the opposite. Truth be told, the Amish are doing quite well these days, thank you very much. That's not to say some Amish people aren't struggling. Some are, but by almost any measure, the Amish in America have done spectacularly well on the material-abundance scale. Amish income and wealth are rising. The Amish keep finding their way into new businesses they were never in before, and the vast majority of these businesses are succeeding. Ninety-five percent, say some estimates, compared to 50 percent of new businesses nationwide. The Amish earn more, keep more and succeed more than most other groups—and that's with the "Amish" tourist trade still dominated by the non-Amish. I guess what I'm trying to say is, please, don't organize any pie sales or throw any telethons for the Amish. The Amish should be donating money to *you.*

There's a whole bunch of factors behind this.

Some of the credit for Amish success goes to how driven and hardworking our people tend to be. There aren't too many lazy Amish. Some of it is how diligently the Amish save. One recent estimate said the Amish, on average, save 20 percent of their income, compared to a national rate of 0 to 5 percent. I know my father always hammered that lesson into my head as a boy, insisting I put aside half of the little money he allowed me to keep from my part-time job earnings "for a rainy day." He never explained why I might need extra money in inclement weather, but as an adult, I save just like he told me to.

The Amish are also loath to take on debt. A typical Amish family will borrow when necessary but only for a clear, productive purpose—and any debt is to be paid off in full as quickly as humanly possible. No high-interest credit cards, no paying just the minimum, no revolving credit plans for my people. You might think that, with so little credit history, the Amish would have trouble getting loans. Exactly the opposite is true. Bankers aren't at all leery of lending to the Amish. The Amish hate debt so much, they tend to pay it off fast and fully—almost never falling into default. All a banker has to do is look at the loan history of a borrower's parents and other relatives to see: There's very little risk in lending to the Amish.

Amish farms might look quiet, bucolic and slow, but truly, some of them are money machines. They don't require much expensive machinery—not when Amish families have six or eight or ten children who all work for free. So no big payments to International Harvester or John Deere. Getting the work done is often just a matter of sending the many children out with pitchforks and milk buckets after giving them a stern talking-to about the character-building importance of performing daily chores.

Taken together, these Amish traditions and character traits have all helped the Amish thrive, but some credit also goes to timing, demographics and luck. The Amish didn't cause farm prices to sky-rocket. That happened on its own—in many of the places where the Amish happened to own property, Pennsylvania and Ohio especially. This is beautiful, open country. God isn't making any more of it. These areas aren't far from major population centers, making them sought-after second-home territory for well-off city people. Lately, I've been seeing mansions being built on million-dollar pieces of land right across the road from the farms and simple homes of Amish families. That's pushed prices up even more.

Any Amish family lucky enough to have bought fifty or seventy-five acres in one of these prime locations decades ago is almost certainly a multimillionaire family now—on paper, anyway.

The Amish population keeps expanding like gangbusters, and many of those Amish children will eventually want farms of their own. That in itself is causing the Amish population to shift around.

In 1960 there were only forty thousand Amish in the United States. In 1980 that number had jumped to eighty thousand. The total population now approaches three hundred thousand spread across twenty-eight states, and it's doubling every twenty years, a nearly unheard-of 5 percent growth rate. Fifteen new Amish settlements are being formed every year. The only real question is whether we cross the one-million mark before or after 2050.

The biggest jumps in numbers aren't where you'd expect to see them. It's places like New York and Missouri and even parts of Canada that have seen the swiftest growth. The more famously Amish-packed Pennsylvania and Ohio, where farmland is so expensive and so hard to find, are holding steady. But huge extended families are always spreading out looking for new places where the next generations can continue their farming tradition.

That rapid growth is hard to ignore. No other group in the United States can match it, and almost all of it comes from inside. We're not seeking converts like the Jehovah's Witnesses, knocking on doors and handing out copies of the *Watchtower*. Hardly any of our growth comes from recruiting. The Amish don't proselytize, and few outsiders are tempted by our lack of modern conveniences or our sense of style. The numbers are all about the large families and a 90 percent post-Rumspringa baptism rate.

Farming is still a big part of the Amish economy, but it isn't the only thing that is putting money into Amish pockets. Not by a long shot. Lately, in fact, agriculture is starting to become less important in the economics of Amish life. The phrase *Amish farmer* used to be almost redundant. But *Amish businessman* could soon take its place.

This is one result of the rising prices for all that farmland the Amish own, the same squeeze that many suburban Americans have experienced as their real estate prices have gone up. When the children get old enough to leave home, marry and start families of their own, they need to make some difficult choices. Many can't afford houses and hundred-acre farms like the ones they grew up on. They're out-of-sight expensive now. And while many families have packed up everything and moved to places that are affordable for the children, others don't want to abandon the church and community their parents, grandparents and great-grandparents have always been a part of. The Amish always think of family first.

So more and more young Amish men and women are finding other ways to support themselves and their families, starting their own businesses especially, including businesses they never would have been allowed to own or work in before.

A generation ago, the devout Amish could only sell products they would actually use themselves—things like hand-sewn quilts, hand-crafted furniture and baked goods. These rules were enforced very strictly. When I was a kid, I sold little wooden bridges that I built out in the yard. That was a typical Amish business. That's all changed now. These days, far more is acceptable, even encouraged.

Even if the dollar signs look tempting, Amish entrepreneurs still won't open businesses the church considers morally objectionable. So don't go looking for the "Plain Peoples' Casino." No "Stoltzfus Gentlemen's Club," either. But the rules are definitely looser now. Amish businesses make and sell high-priced desk toys, designer leather clothing and other items the owners probably wouldn't use themselves.

In their new businesses, the Amish still rely on some of the old techniques: humble bosses, hand-craftsmanship, a life-work balance that says, "Family first." But as the rules get looser, Amish business-people are gaining more and more of the tools to compete in the larger, outside world. Amish businesspeople now routinely use cell phones, inventory computers, electronic cash registers. Increasingly, they are installing air-conditioning in their stores. This is still a deli-cate topic. Are Amish business owners putting too much emphasis on the business and too little on the Amish? Some bishops think so, some Amish people think so, and many tourists visiting the Amish stores are confused. That's why you'll often hear an Amish business-man pointing out that the air-conditioning or the electric lights are running on solar or wind power.

Myron Miller is a perfect example of this off-the-farm phenom-enon. As he reached adulthood two decades ago in Millersburg, Ohio, he thought about farming. Land in the area was already pricey back then—good luck today!—so Myron started building furniture instead. Now he has two companies: Four Corners Furniture sells retail to the public, and Miller Bedroom Wholesale sells to seventy-five distributors around the country. Myron has a dozen work-ers already and sees no end to the growth. He did all this with his eighth-grade education and certainly no MBA from the University of Pennsylvania's Wharton School. "I run my business according to God's way and plan," he says. Though he isn't directly in the tourist business, he has benefited from all the visitors. "I saw all the tourism coming in—we're blessed to be the number one tourism attraction in Ohio—and so I thought I'd try to go into that, selling furniture to the tourists. Then I realized that was just the tip of the iceberg. I thought I'd spread my wings and market the furniture elsewhere."

He certainly did, setting an example for other Amish entrepreneurs, who keep coming up with bigger and better and more profitable business ideas.

Take Leon Stoltzfus, who owns the Groffdale Machine Company in Leola, my old Rumspringa stomping grounds. Leon's making a lot of money manufacturing surprisingly sleek and colorful products that are bought by local Amish people. At first glance, his Lancaster County place of business looks like any farm, complete with cows and large fields of crops. When the doors are open, a closer look shows a thriving, high-tech business making some of the best twenty-inch, spoke-wheel scooters on the market today. Amish aren't allowed to ride bicycles. They were forbidden in the 1890s as unacceptably worldly. Since the first modern scooter patents didn't come until the 1920s, they were not included in the ban. They could be fast and any color at all, the perfect alternative to the bikes of the era. Inside the Groffdale plant, you can see Amish employees working on various stages of partially built kick scooters in a huge array of colors from red to yellow to bright pink. Word around the county is that Leon has annual sales of $1.5 million.

That buys a lot of scrapple, I'd think.

CHAPTER 21
SUNSHINE STATE OF MIND

You want another sign of growing Amish affluence? The Amish, like other groups with money, are now being targeted in what some people call big-dollar scams.

While the Amish are good savers, they can be really dumb investors, especially when they get into financial territory they aren't familiar with. Since they do have money, they can be ripe targets.

A businessman named Tim Moffitt, who'd sold his Super Fruit produce company in Chambersburg, Pennsylvania, next proposed a luxury RV park an hour north of Orlando. He targeted a pool of investors that you'd never associate with the world of recreational camping vehicles. He approached eighty Amish families and was able to raise $15 to $20 million.

There's a lot of controversy about Moffitt's plans. Unfortunately, the park still isn't built, and investigators wonder if it ever will be. For now, at least, most of the Amish families haven't demanded their money back. They're being loyal, they say. Moffitt isn't Amish, but he's well-known by the Amish, which is how he managed to raise so much money with just his word that the deal would be lucrative.

Then there is Monroe Beachy. He's a white-haired, bearded member of an Amish church in Sugarcreek, Ohio, who admitted defrauding 2,600 of his own Amish people in 29 states out of nearly $17 million.

You've probably heard of Bernie Madoff and his Ponzi schemes. Beachy was the Amish Madoff and just as despicable. Beginning in 2006, he promised to hold the Amish investors' money in safe investments while actually putting the funds into far riskier securities. He was indicted, of course. "Beachy told the investors that their money would be used to purchase risk-free US government securities, which would generate returns for the investors," the Securities and Exchange Commission said last year in a civil filing. "In reality, Beachy used the money to make speculative investments in high yield (junk) bonds, mutual funds, and stocks."

Eventually, when things started to spiral out of control, Beachy did the unthinkable for any self-respecting Amish man. He filed for bankruptcy, officially asking the US Bankruptcy Court to figure out which if any of the creditors would get paid. That got people even more riled up than the missing millions. The investors didn't just fume, they wrote hundreds of letters asking that they be allowed to handle things in their own way. The court denied their requests.

One woman lamented her losses, but she was refusing any help from the government. Her savings before her unfortunate decision to invest had been meager, she said, but she'd put what she could into "the Amish Bank of Monroe Beachy."

The Amish looked at people like her and did exactly what you'd expect them to do. They set up a fund that members of the community could contribute to, and they helped the defrauded people as much as they could.

Without a doubt, the Amish are finding new, worldly ways to enjoy their material blessings. Gradually, Amish homes are getting larger and better appointed. Cars, once forsaken entirely or at least hidden in English neighbors' barns, are now more often parked openly on Amish farms. The makes and models are getting fancier, too.

It's more than cars. Since I was old enough to see one in the backyard of an English home, I'd never heard of any Amish having a swimming pool. They're forbidden, but more and more homes include lined, man-made swimming ponds, complete with slides and diving boards. And more and more Amish parents are taking the kids out to dinner. Yes, in restaurants! We *never* did that when I was a kid!

The elders aren't happy with all this modernization. Sometimes, the bishops still issue objections to these changes. But more often these days, it's compliments.

"Nice tractor, Calvin!"

And then there is Pinecraft, Florida.

Nestled at the eastern edge of Sarasota, Pinecraft began its life as a tourist camp in the 1920s. Now, based entirely on word of mouth, the compact community of Pinecraft has morphed into a major vacation destination for the Amish. That's right, vacationing Amish. Five thousand people visit every winter, some coming down for a week or two, many staying through the season.

The visitors stroll around in traditional Amish clothing—the men in black hats, the women in white bonnets, now protecting their faces from the bright Florida sun's dangerous UV rays. The Amish snowbirds settle into rental houses on streets named for well-known Amish families—Kaufman, Schrock, Yoder. The Amish truly have made the place their own. The way New Yorkers have Miami and Fort Lauderdale, the way Chicagoans winter in Fort Myers and St. Petersburg, the Amish pilgrims keep turning up in Pinecraft.

They don't come by horse-and-buggy, of course. That ride could take 'til March. Hopping a plane to Sarasota Bradenton International Airport would be the quickest way to get there, but that isn't what the Amish do. Flying, though quietly permitted in genuine emergencies, is considered too worldly, too much of a luxury, for a flock of Amish snowbirds. In the eyes of most bishops, flying can't be considered essential when chartered Pioneer buses and their English drivers are making express runs to Pinecraft every day. The Amish head south for the same reasons people have always visited Florida in the winter. The sun is shining, the temperatures are pleasant, the whole lifestyle is a little more relaxed. The sunsets at Lido Beach are to die for. And it's really, really, really cold back home. Plus, if any more excuse is needed, how much farming can anyone do when snow is piled up on the ground?

Like most of Florida, Pinecraft is dotted with palm trees and trailer parks, but the telltale signs of the Amish are everywhere, too. The Laundromat has clotheslines. (Bring your own pins.) Yoder's Restaurant serves peanut-butter-pie pancakes topped with homemade whipped cream. Copies of the *Budget*, the 125-year-old Amish newspaper, are shipped in weekly and passed around. On the shuf-fleboard courts at Pinecraft Park, one lane is "Reserved for Ladies," the sign says. But with most of the bishops so far away, the rules of Amish living are a whole lot looser there.

Cell phones are used far more openly. From time to time, even cameras come out. Almost everyone uses electricity in their homes. Up north, most traditional Amish people do not ride bikes. They are only allowed to use push scooters. But in Pinecraft, oversized three-wheel bicycles are everywhere. There's even a solar-powered buggy rolling around town—no horse at all. From Pinecraft, buses take the young people to Siesta Key Beach, where some of them actually wear bathing suits—even the occasional bikini! You certainly wouldn't see that back home. But most sunbathers do stay in their traditional long dresses or long dark pants while lounging in low-slung beach chairs or playing beach volleyball.

Here's something else you won't see up north: Many of the houses—simple, wood-framed cottages and Spanish-style mini-villas—feature hand-carved signs with the owners' family name. That would be seen as highly boastful in the Amish north. In Pine-craft, people enjoy seeing who the owners are. No matter how simple or fancy the homes in Pinecraft are, one thing they aren't is cheap. Recently, a tiny six-hundred-square-foot bungalow on Graber Avenue, right next door to an ice-cream shop, was listed for $229,000. That may not sound expensive to people who live in New York or San Francisco or even suburban Lancaster, but it makes Pinecraft one of the most expensive communities in Sara-sota County, which is itself one of the priciest places to live in Florida. And the Amish almost always buy their vacation homes with cash.

No one asks too many questions in Pinecraft, and no one offers many answers. Everyone just tries to blend in as well as they can. One of the good things about Pinecraft is that Amish visitors get a chance to meet Amish people from other states. For people who don't get around too much, it's a rare opportunity to trade local attitudes and compare far-flung Ordnungs.

Typical Pinecraft conversation:

"Your bishop allows cell phones?"

"He does."

"Really? My bishop hardly allows speaking in a loud voice!"

Pinecraft even has its own Internet blogger to record the details and keep everyone in the loop. "All these groups can mingle down here in a way they wouldn't at home," says Katie Troyer, who left the church but still very much embraces Amish culture. "That's a puzzle people have been trying to figure out for ages." Always riding her three-wheeler with a camera, she posts her photos and reports at Pinecraft-Sarasota.Blogspot.com.

"What happens in Pinecraft stays in Pinecraft," she jokes—unless you happen to see it on Katie's blog!

I'm really not sure why the Amish rules should be any different in Florida than they are anywhere else. Why are bicycles and electricity the devil's implements in Pennsylvania but perfectly okay in Florida? The last time I checked, we had the same God in both places. Does heaven have a southern division with different rules? If it's okay in Florida to live like Mennonites, why not carry that back home?

To me, it's just another example of Amish hypocrisy. Always read the Bible literally unless you're south of Washington, DC!

I've been to Pinecraft three or four times. The truth is, it really isn't my idea of a great vacation spot. Shuffleboard at the park! Black hats in the sunshine! Gabbing at the local diner all day! There's a saying about Pinecraft that's always rung true to me: It's for the newlyweds and nearly deads and no one else! For my money, vacations are about going somewhere different and experiencing something new. I love to travel. I love sightseeing and going new places and meeting new people and soaking in the great outdoors. I've gone hunting in Colorado, where I got an elk. I've been hunting and fishing in Canada, where I got a bear and caught my limit of walleye. I've been to Yellowstone, the Grand Tetons. I hiked to the bottom of the Grand Canyon and camped down there. That's my idea of getting away from it all, five thousand feet down! I've been on a couple of cruises. I love camping out at country-music festivals like Ohio's Jamboree in the Hills. I hit Ocean Beach, Maryland, at least once a year. I've visited the Dominican Republic and Cancún. I made a mission trip with my church to Zambia in Africa. Now, that was amazing! We helped build houses for the people, and I even did a three-hundred-foot bungee jump at Victoria Falls. A couple of my friends told me that might not be wise.

"Has anybody died?" I asked the guy strapping in the tourists.

"Not yet," he said.

I'm not sure if that was supposed to calm me, but I jumped, and I lived.

The only trip I really didn't enjoy was my first visit to Myrtle Beach. I was twenty years old, too young to get into the local bars. I hung out on the beach all day with the young crowd. I'd been working inside that year, framing sheds. My skin was pale as fresh milk, and I got such a horrible sunburn, I spent the rest of the trip moaning in the motel room. I swore I'd never go back, but I did the following summer. I was legal then, and the local bars were a blast. I didn't step on the beach a single time. It was a huge improvement.

CHAPTER 22
EXES

An Amish race-car driver . . . an Amish police officer . . . an Amish nurse. You think I'm joking? You should meet Marlin Yoder, Elsie Keim and Naomi Kramer. People raised in traditional Amish families end up in all kinds of places you wouldn't expect.

It turns out I am not alone in beating my own unique path through Amish Country. I'm certainly not the only person of my background who lives with one foot in the Amish community and one foot outside. It's that closeness *and* that distance that make me who I am. Though I remain a work in progress, you know what? These days, I kinda like who I am.

People like me have all felt frustration with the Amish life we were born into: the lack of freedom, the pressure to conform, the unfashionable headwear. At the same time, most of us never really get the Amish out of our blood. It's part of what defines us, always. As we've gone into the outside world and expanded our horizons, we haven't lost our Amish-ness at all, we've added to it. That's how I like to think of it, anyway.

My part of Pennsylvania is crawling with people like me, as are the Amish strongholds in Ohio, Indiana, Wisconsin and other states. We love the Amish. We admire the Amish. We are part of the Amish community. We protect the Amish in whatever ways we can, and now we are uniquely situated to understand these inward-looking communities—and to help them—without surrendering our own free judgment or personal choice.

Those who walk this road with me I consider my brothers and sisters in arms. I am so proud of how far they have traveled, what obstacles they have overcome, what special lives they have built for themselves and their families. Some still live quietly, farming, working construction, owning businesses, becoming valued and respected members of small communities. Others are roaring into the outside world, caution be damned.

I am thinking of people like Marlin Yoder. Marlin came from the tiny Amish enclave of Richland Center, Wisconsin. Just a few short years ago, his idea of speed was a galloping horse. Now he's turning laps at two hundred miles an hour and working his way into a car-racing career. He isn't slapping reins anymore. He's pedal-to-the-metal now.

Marlin caught the NASCAR bug listening to races on a smuggled radio hidden beneath a mattress in his family's Amish home. Apparently, my older brothers weren't the only Amish teenagers sneaking radios in and out of the house. Marlin slipped away and learned to race on the same go-kart tracks that launched driving stars such as Danica Patrick. These days, Marlin's all about speed and competition and winning, an almost total U-turn from the poky humility of his Amish upbringing. He's committed to the racer's life now, even though his mother still doesn't understand.

"I know she misses me," Marlin says, "but after you talk with her for ten or fifteen minutes, she's still asking me why I don't come back. They truly believe that if I was to die today, I'd burn in hell."

Verna Gillen drives a slower vehicle but a much bigger and heavier one. Raised on an Amish farm outside the auction town of Kidron, Ohio, she couldn't see spending the rest of her life with her fingers in the dirt. "On my fortieth birthday," she says, "I thought, 'You know what? It's now or never.'" Her five kids were grown. She had gotten divorced, had moved around a bit and was married to a new man who was a trucker. "Why not?" she asked herself. She took a training course and got herself hired by Old Dominion Freight Line in Indianapolis as an over-the-road big-rig driver. Her first year on the job, she was named rookie of the year at the Indiana Truck Driving Championship. She took first place in the twin-bed category, the first woman ever to score so high in seventy-five years. Now, five nights a week, she's driving a day-cab ten-speed tractor-trailer from Indianapolis to Rock Island, Illinois, with a healthy salad and a piece of fruit in the cab. In Rock Island, she meets a driver from Des Moines, Iowa. They swap freight loads, and she heads back home.

"I keep moving," she says, something she certainly wasn't brought up to do, at least not at distances like these.

To me, Elsie Keim is an inspiration and a hero.

Growing up on an Amish farm in Ohio, she knew full well what was waiting for her next as an Amish wife and mother: the quiet, slow, traditional way. That might be fine for many Amish girls, she figured, but it wasn't right for her.

"I'm an adrenaline junkie," Elsie says.

That wasn't too popular at home.

Her parents shunned her when she turned eighteen and started driving. She moved to Florida for most of that year. When she got back to Ohio, her parents barely spoke to her. They told her she was surely going to hell.

Looking for a life that better suited her, Elsie moved to Arizona and got herself admitted to the police academy in Mesa, a sprawling suburb east of Phoenix with 450,000 people in 133 square miles. You couldn't patrol that with a horse-and-buggy. Now she drives a black-and-white patrol car through modern neighborhoods, sworn to protect and to serve. "I'm the oddball," she says. "I like to go to the extreme."

To Elsie, that means more than writing tickets and making arrests. She looks back at her Amish heritage and learns from it. "I understand you can't change anybody overnight, but I can shed a little light on them. I want to leave them better."

Adds Elsie: "I have a mission. This isn't a job."

That's about how Ray Beechy feels. His whole life has been about overcoming obstacles. When he was twelve years old, his left arm had to be cut off below the elbow after an accident in his Amish father's sawmill. "It's never kept me from much of anything other than shuffling cards or clapping," Ray says with a smile. It wasn't going to keep him from riding bulls. "I was sixteen when I really took an interest in the rodeo circuit," he said. "A friend of mine that lived close by was riding bulls at the time and got me interested." Ray thought it looked like fun.

His Amish upbringing helps him stay calm at the highest-tension moments of the sport. "You don't think about the ride until you nod your head. I try to think about anything other than bull riding right before I go to the chutes."

Now all he wants to do is keep riding and expand the sport of rodeo around his home in Hammond, Illinois, to bring more young people into the sport he loves. "I want to get on as many bulls and win as much money as I can," he says.

You'll notice what's missing here, as we survey the unexpected achievements of people brought up Amish: professional occupations. Doctors, lawyers, bankers, accountants, professors—jobs that require college and graduate degrees. Whatever talent and drive they may be blessed with, Amish children are largely excluded from positions like those. Blame their lack of education. The vast majority of Amish kids don't even attend high school. Suit-and-tie jobs are almost unthinkable. I know the American promise that anyone can grow up to be president of the United States, but I'm pretty sure the country isn't going to elect a president with an eighth-grade education any time soon.

That's a huge disadvantage in the outside world. Most groups celebrate the professional achievements of their members: the first black doctor in town, the first female CEO. The Amish celebrate an 85 or 90 percent retention rate, and Amish children without high school educations keep doing what their parents and grandparents did.

Honestly, what else are most of them prepared for?

This is part of the reason, I believe, that so many Amish people who leave the community eventually come back home. What exactly are they prepared to do in the outside world? Socially awkward, lacking education, disconnected from the advances of modern life: Does that sound like someone with strong job prospects? What do they put on their résumés? Proficiency with nineteenth-century farm implements? Valedictorian of eighth grade? Good luck explaining that in the interview!

This precise issue is what motivated four college-goers, all raised Amish, to start the Amish Descendant Scholarship Fund. William Troyer, Saloma Furlong and cousins Naomi Kramer and Emma Miller knew how hard it was to get their educations. Working with the Mennonite Church, they are hoping to help other ex-Amish get theirs, as well.

"The parents are not supportive of them getting their education," said Emma, who left the Amish when she was sixteen. She worked hard and graduated from San Diego State University and then entered a master's program in economics at London Metropolitan University. But many ex-Amish who might have dreams of higher education find they can't get student loans and grants to help with the tuition. Their parents won't sign the application forms.

"My decision to leave the Amish and go to college was obviously not what my parents had wished for me," Emma said. "So for the first three years, I did not get any financial help."

Her cousin Naomi had a similar experience. Raised Amish in Jamesport, Missouri, she started working in a bakery when she was thirteen. By nineteen, she said, "I had a feeling of discontent. The next stop for me was to get married and settle down, but I wanted to see the world. I felt called to do something more." She moved to Florida, began working at a nursing home, earned her GED, and dreamed of becoming a nurse.

With the help of a generous donor who was inspired by her gritty story, Naomi earned her degree at Goshen College with high honors.

Commencement day, even her parents showed up, looking proud.

"It feels like a really good accomplishment," she says. "Amish women are raised to be nurturing. It was rooted in me that my role should be as a housewife and mother. I've really liked that I've been able to be nurturing in my career."

Frankly, I also feel proud of the distance I have come.

When I was a little boy, running around the farm first in Lancaster County, then later in Lebanon County, getting my eight years of schooling, being groomed to live the Amish life, I don't think too many people would have ever predicted that I'd be where I am today. No one could possibly have expected a child who grew up without a television (except when his teenage brothers finally snuck one in) to become the star of a popular television show! I never expected that. I'm sure my family, friends and church never did. I couldn't even have formed the idea in my head. But look at me now. I really do have a life I feel I was destined for.

PART III
BRINGING IT ALL BACK HOME

CHAPTER 23
CATCHING UP

The real stories of Amish life have a way of never quite ending. Let me get you get up to speed on what's become of some of the unique people involved.

Fannie and Delila Miller are doing remarkably well now, safe with their family in Heuvelton, New York, putting the trauma of their roadside kidnapping mostly behind them. Valentine Byler, the man who kept the Amish out of Social Security, remains unsung and largely forgotten. Carrying on in Byler's spirit, however, some Amish are seeking exemption from Obamacare. The clapers are still at it, just as obnoxious as ever, though thankfully they haven't killed anyone lately while throwing rocks at Amish buggies.

Pennsylvania's crackdown on puppy mills has forced some Amish out of that sordid business—or have they just gone underground? Animal activists say that poorly bred mill puppies are still flooding America's pet stores.

An appellate court in Cincinnati overturned Sam Mullet's hate-crimes conviction. The judges didn't dispute that the beard attacks occurred or that the iron-fisted bishop was behind them, but ruled that the "Barber of Bergholz" and his scissor-wielding followers were not motivated primarily by anti-Amish bias. "Faith permeates most, if not all, aspects of life in the Amish community," the judges wrote in a 2–1 decision. Still, "Interpersonal and intrafamily disagreements, not the victims' religious beliefs, sparked the attacks."

Since the bishop was still convicted on other counts, he failed to win an immediate release from federal prison.

Even as Mullet sat in federal prison in Texarkana, Texas, there were signs that he still had a firm grip on his loyal followers. One of his grandsons, Dan Shrock, said the bishop was still running his eight-hundred-acre compound from prison. "Sam Mullet's community is a cult. They don't have freedom," the young man said. "He has power over people's minds, gets them to do things he wants them to do and believe in him. I've been there, my cousins have been there, and we know it, and it is true."

In a rare interview, the bishop's wife insisted her husband and his followers were being treated unfairly because of their unconventional lifestyle and conservative views. "They just want to talk about what we did," Martha Mullet said. "Nobody talks about what happened to us. Nobody talks about the root of the problem."

She never stopped defending the man she was married to for forty-nine years. "He's a very gentle, loving man," she said. "And yes, he can get stern, just like anybody else, but people say he has power. No, I don't feel he does have power."

But two months after that interview, the bishop's wife died suddenly from cardiac arrest. The court refused Sam Mullet's request for an emergency furlough from prison to attend the funeral in Ohio.

While the couple's 18 children and 110 grandchildren grieved, there was one thing the Mullet family didn't have to worry about:

money. The family sold oil and gas fracking rights to their compound in Bergholz in a multimillion-dollar deal that saved the farm. As his appeal presses on, he may forfeit his public defender and lose some of that easy money paying future legal bills.

None of this, however, has calmed the concerns of the bishop's grandson. "I still worry a lot about my family," Dan Shrock said.

The question of drug abuse still lingers heavily over Amish Country.

In the years after the Pagan-Amish drug bust, many parents kept insisting that drug abuse wasn't a real problem in the Amish community. Just a few troubled kids, they said, and those sad cases could be dealt with quietly. Despite the vivid stories from the courtroom and in the media, most people slipped right back to the old, familiar denials. Drugs? Here? No way! Then, in May 2002, a documentary film called *Devil's Playground* aired on the cable channel Cinemax. Shot on location in LaGrange and Elkhart, Indiana, the movie portrayed rampant drug and alcohol use among Amish teenagers and young adults. All of a sudden, parents were alarmed, and young Amish druggies were a hot topic again.

In September of that year, Norm Kauffmann, town manager of Shipshewana, Indiana, called a meeting of Amish parents to discuss issues raised by the film. Shipshewana, just outside LaGrange, is home to the third-largest Amish community in America.

While most of the parents in the room said the movie exaggerated the problem, almost everyone agreed there *was* a problem— and it definitely needed a fresh response. Out of that conversation grew the Amish Youth Vision Project, a unique set of initiatives that have kept the Indiana Amish ahead of most other Amish communities in facing the drug issue.

The bad news is that the problem hasn't gone away yet. The good news is that caring people are still fighting the good fight every day with a distinctly Amish approach. Traditional treatment programs like DARE would never work with Amish kids, in part because they come to drugging and drinking in their own uniquely Amish ways.

"Most programs assume a gradual trajectory into alcohol and drug use," says James Cates, one of Youth Vision's founders, "a stolen cigarette here or there, a beer or two on the sly. They do not assume the first experience will be a party with peers at age sixteen, which may last all night and involve heavy drinking, and that this can be the norm for drinking for several years."

Thanks, Rumspringa!

"The Amish learn at a very early age to keep a flat expression and not portray emotion when they're dealing with the English and they're uncertain," Cates says. "It takes someone who's Amish and been around it for years to be able to interpret what's going on behind the mask." Since there are no Amish doctors or psychotherapists, the group counseling sessions are led by English therapists. But each session is co-led by an already baptized young Amish person. The combination has proven highly effective.

Don't go looking for a memorial plaque at the site of the old West Nickel Mines School. The property is open pasture now, where horses graze and five flowering pear trees stand in silent tribute to what happened there. That's the only hint of the horror of October 2, 2006, when a deeply tormented man shot five Amish schoolgirls to death and wounded five others before taking his own life. For almost a decade now, children from the area have been attending the New Hope Amish School. It is equipped with sensors that will alert the teacher to any visitors. The driveway is paved, making it the first Amish school in Lancaster County that doesn't have a dirt or gravel entrance.

"Each one of the kids remembered the shooter spinning his tires and the sound of gravel moving under the wheels," said John Coldiron, a local zoning official. "Everyone decided the kids wouldn't have to deal with that sound again." Another thing that makes this new school unlike any other Amish school I've ever seen is that the front door has a lock on it. But even so, the building hasn't really become a fortress. That would be its own kind of defeat.

The dead girls have never been forgotten, of course, and probably never will be: Naomi Ebersol, Lena Miller, Mary Miller, Anna Stoltzfus and Marian Stoltzfus Fisher, the thirteen-year-old who said, "Shoot me first." The injured carry on with stories of triumph and tragedy. Barbie Fisher, Marian's eleven-year-old sister who said, "Shoot me second," had lingering issues with her right arm. But after shoulder surgery, she was strong enough to pitch in softball games again.

Esther King, who was thirteen at the time, returned to school in the months after the shooting, graduated and has been working on the family farm. Rachel Stoltzfus, eight years old when she was shot, also returned to school and now seems to be thriving. Sarah Stoltzfus, who was twelve at the time, had the most miraculous recovery. With a bullet lodged in the side of her brain, she was not expected to survive. But she got better quickly and returned to school. Her last serious symptom was impaired vision in her left eye. But even that cleared up over time.

The youngest victim, Rosanna King, who was six years old when the shooter entered the schoolhouse, has had the toughest road. She too was shot in the head. Her brain injury was so severe, she was removed from life support at the Milton S. Hershey Medical Center and sent home to be with her family. But all these years later, surrounded at home by her mother, father, sisters and brothers, she presses on. She does not walk or talk. She has frequent seizures. But she sits up in a wheelchair and seems to recognize family members. Among the regular volunteers who still help with her care is Terri Roberts, the mother of shooter Charlie Roberts. She has become a familiar presence in the victims' families' lives. A tall, thin woman with spiky gray hair, she comes to the Kings' house most Thursdays, helping to bathe Rosanna and read her stories.

Her enduring presence in this circle of tragedy seems to bring comfort to everyone.

Money poured into the fund that was created after the school shooting, more than five million dollars. Some of it came from well-off donors. Twenty African churches donated one dollar each. The money continues to cover medical costs and physical therapy. Some of it helped the Kings outfit their farmhouse to accommodate Rosanna's wheelchair. Though the donations eventually slowed to a trickle, some donors have named the Nickel Mines Accountability Committee in their wills.

In the years since the shooting, the families of the victims have continued to be strong voices for forgiveness and peace. So has Terri Roberts. She and the children's parents speak at meetings and conferences. They've hosted psychologists from Russia and religious leaders from Israel and help others confront senseless tragedy around the world. They have reached out to the families at Virginia Tech,

Sandy Hook and other mass school shootings. They talk about ready access to firearms. They discuss the culture of violence in America. They describe the awesome power of forgiveness, something they know a lot about. Each place they've been, they've tried to remind everyone that the family of the perpetrator often suffers as much as the families of the victims, perhaps even more so. Either way, they are locked in tragedy together.

The shooter's mother opens almost every talk the same way. "Our son Charles was responsible for the Nickel Mines tragedy," she says, her voice often quaking as she relives the horror. She always ends on a hopeful note with a lesson she learned from her Amish neighbors: "We need to allow forgiveness in our hearts so we can be whole."

It's a lesson, Terri Roberts says, she has finally made her own.

"I have found a lot of people want to focus on the darkest day in their life instead of all the good that there is," she says. "Through God's grace, I feel that we can move forward in anything in life, no matter how dark our darkest day is."

CHAPTER 24
KELLY'S GIRL

The story of Kelly McGillis's *Witness* visit stuck with our family for a very long time. Given how jumpy the Amish are about outside attention, you knew someone would have to object to her unexpected appearance in our lives.

Someone did.

Our bishop, Sammie Kaufman.

Kelly came to us through an English neighbor who was working with the movie people. He knew how eager she was to learn first-hand about the Amish. After Kelly had been with us a few days, planting crooked rows of potatoes and copying my mother's Pennsylvania Dutch accent, the actress's photo ran on the front page of the local newspaper, the *Intelligencer Journal*. That afternoon, Bishop Kaufman showed up at our house.

"She cannot stay here," the bishop told my mother.

My mom was a naturally hospitable woman. She'd been happy to welcome the curious visitor from Hollywood, pleased to open our home and share our lives with her. Kelly couldn't have been a better-behaved guest. She seemed genuinely charmed by us and respectful toward our culture. She explained that her character in the movie, Rachel Lapp, was an Amish widow whose son had witnessed a murder. Harrison Ford was her co-star, she said, and he'd been "Indiana Jones" and "Han Solo." Those names meant nothing to our Amish family. But this Mr. Ford, it seemed, would be playing the detective trying to solve the murder that the Amish boy saw. Kelly wanted her portrayal to be as real as she could possibly make it.

The bishop was having none of it.

"She's an *actress*," he said, the word coming out as if he had said *heathen* or *adulterer*. "You know what actresses do."

My mother looked at him and said nothing.

"They call attention to themselves," the bishop said. "Sometimes with millions of people watching." In the bishop's view, I suppose that was almost a mortal sin.

Bishop Kaufman and the other local bishops, it seemed, had decided to forbid all the Amish people of south central Pennsylvania from cooperating with *Witness* in any way. No renting property to the location scouts. No taking work as set builders or horse wranglers. No appearing as extras in the film.

The local Amish leaders didn't seem to have any particular objection to the movie's premise, script, cast or crew. The problem seemed to be that these Hollywood people had come to Pennsylvania Amish Country to make a movie set in the world of the Amish. That they couldn't abide.

"This is not something we can support," the bishop said.

My mother was sad to hear that. She hadn't meant to offend anyone. Kelly was gracious and understanding when my mother explained to her what the bishop had said. "I don't want to get you or your family in trouble," she told my mother as she collected her things to leave.

They agreed to stay in touch amid the thank-yous and the good-byes.

The movie production continued all around us. Actors were hired for all the Amish roles. The famous barn-building scene was filmed on a farm owned by an English family, right across the road from our house. When the movie was ready for release, it had its world premiere at the Fulton Opera House in Lancaster. This was a very big deal. A searchlight swept the sky over Lancaster. The arriving stars and dignitaries climbed out of limousines and walked a red carpet on North Prince Street. Governor Dick Thornburgh was there. He was a Pennsylvania governor who supported Amish-themed productions instead of issuing statements against them. Many other local politicians and civic leaders came. The hometown crowd was wildly enthusiastic. Harrison Ford didn't make it. He was off somewhere filming another movie, but Kelly McGillis came. Everyone said she looked beautiful, and even some of the Amish noticed that.

Several of the out-of-town movie critics commented on her Pennsylvania Dutch accent in the film. They said her speech sounded highly authentic, and I think I know why. Kelly said that my mother had been a great role model, and she also told a reporter that "the youngest child, a four-year-old, spoke only Dutch. So it was a great learning experience trying to communicate with him." I knew I was that four-year-old. Most of the critics, including the one from the *Philadelphia Inquirer*, really liked the film. I've seen it quite a few times since it first came out. I've liked it every time. The movie starring our houseguest was a blockbuster hit.

We stayed in touch with Kelly over the years. She had a huge burst of fame in the late 1980s, and not just for *Witness*. She had leading roles in *Top Gun* with Tom Cruise and *The Accused* with Jodie Foster. One critic called her "a siren with brains." I'll bet she liked that. For a while there, Kelly McGillis, our sweet boarder, was one of the top young actresses in Hollywood. Then her fame faded, as fame often does. She stopped getting big-budget roles. After living for a while in Key West, Florida, she moved to the tiny town of Mohnton in Berks County, Pennsylvania, a short drive north of Lancaster, where she lived quietly in a five-bedroom 1910 farmhouse and supported local theater. One night, she gave a talk at EPAC, the Ephrata Performing Arts Center, a fund-raiser for the community-theater group. She spoke with real candor about her life.

"When I was doing *Witness*," she said, "I was so scared, I started drinking. I was in a movie opposite Harrison freakin' Ford, Indiana Jones, and I was terrified all the time. I think God brought me back here for a do-over."

After several tries, she told the audience, she had managed to quit drinking. She'd gotten divorced for the second time. She had a great relationship, she said, with her two grown daughters, Kelsey and Sonora. She'd been working with substance abusers at a halfway house. She was much calmer now, she said, taking only occasional acting jobs. She had just turned fifty.

"I still love acting," she said that night. "But now I know it's acting. It's no longer life-and-death to me."

When it came time for questions, my brother Samuel stood up.

"Do you remember me?" he asked.

Kelly smiled and said of course she did.

He reminded her how they had such fun on the farm together and what happened with the bishop. "The Amish bishop came and told us you had to go because you were an actress," my brother told Kelly and the audience, many of whom had never the story. "And during the barn-raising scene, right across from our farm in Strasburg, you took me and my brother down to your camper to have a beer."

Actually, I had never heard that part before. Kelly, perhaps just being discreet, said she didn't remember anything about it.

"I thought maybe after *Witness*," Samuel said, "you might come back and marry an Amish man."

Well, that was not going to happen now, though not for any of the reasons my brother might have suspected. The following year, Kelly came out as a lesbian. She said her sexuality was something she'd been coming to grips with since she was twelve years old. Now she'd found a woman to share her life with. Melanie was her name. She worked as a sales executive in Philadelphia.

After a long, winding journey, Kelly's life seemed like it had finally stabilized. Knowing some of the difficult times she'd been through, hearing about her new balance made me feel really happy for her. My brothers were happy, too. As far we were concerned, she was a wonderful person who deserved all good things—*even if she was an actress*! Two years later, Samuel was thrilled when, one day out of the blue, he got a call from Kelly. She asked if it would be okay if she came by for a visit.

"Love to see you," Samuel told her. "So would my mother." They laughed about not telling the bishop she was coming by.

When she showed up, Kelly was her usual open, friendly self. She asked about the family and told my mother how young she looked. She asked how my mother could've possibly kept up with fifteen children. "Two's enough for me," Kelly said with a laugh.

She said she had some good news she wanted to share: She was getting married and she wanted us to be there. "We'll have a nice reception," she said. "I'd be honored if you guys could come."

"We'd love to," my mother said before Kelly ever had a chance to mention who her spouse-to-be was. "That's so kind of you."

Everyone was happily catching up, and Kelly didn't get into specifics about who she was marrying. I guess my mother, in all her enthusiasm, didn't think to ask. She was just thrilled about Kelly's good fortune. Even after Kelly left that day, Samuel and I never brought up the topic. Why complicate things with a debate over modern marriage? Love is love, and my mother loved Kelly, even if the Amish church was still nowhere close to officially blessing same-sex unions.

Samuel and I talked about it. We decided—I'm not sure if this was right or not, but it's what we decided—we wouldn't lay any of this out for our mother. We'd just take her to Kelly's celebration and let her see for herself.

Sadly, Samuel got a call from Kelly a few weeks later, saying the big event had been postponed. I don't know all the details, but Kelly has since moved to North Carolina, where she's teaching acting, I hear, and doing well. My sweet Amish mother still doesn't realize how close she came to her first gay commitment ceremony.

CHAPTER 25
LAST LAUGH

The uproar over *Amish Mafia* didn't start with Governor Corbett. It didn't end with him, either. Pennsylvania's two US senators, Pat Toomey and Robert Casey, also jumped onto the trash-Levi train, though the petition they signed stopped short of demanding the show be banned or canceled. Frankly, I was waiting for one of them to say I should be jailed. Various other lesser politicians also scrambled aboard—the lieutenant governor, a couple of copycat congressmen, some third-string state legislators.

I guess all of them needed an issue, and I was standing there.

The minute these puppet politicians started talking, I knew someone else had to be pulling their strings. They hadn't all just decided at the exact same moment to come roaring out at me. Why were they suddenly so agitated, almost four seasons into our Discovery Channel run? Whose invisible hand was making their lips move? The Amish aren't known as big voters, so this wasn't about a swing constituency, and most of these so-called public servants had never before shown much interest in Amish sensitivities. I vowed to find out.

I know a lot of people in Amish Country. I did what I always do when I need information. I started asking around. It didn't take long. Three or four names kept coming up, usual suspects from the Amish-tourism industry—plus a couple of irritating busybodies along for the ride. While the politicians were signing petitions and putting out statements, these were the people who seemed to be doing the scut work. Every last one of them, one way or the other, was in the Amish-promotion business, and they were all deeply invested in the old Amish fairy tale.

There was Tom Baldrige from the Lancaster Chamber of Commerce, Kathleen Frankford from the Pennsylvania Dutch Convention & Visitors Bureau, and Donald Kraybill, a professor at Elizabethtown College and widely quoted "Amish expert." Most of all, there was Mary Haverstick, a local videographer who had a Facebook page called Lancastrians Against Amish-sploitation Films and TV Shows. Snappy name, huh? She also had a website, RespectAmish.org. It was hard to say how many people Haverstick represented, if any, but she'd definitely been busy stirring up complaints about our plainspoken TV show. Her group was "dedicated to countering the false 'reality' our region is being depicted [sic] on TV & promoting harmony with our Amish neighbors," she said in a Twitter post.

These were the people who had drawn up the statements the politicians had signed. Their fingerprints were all over the entire attack campaign. Now these back-room advocates were trying to turn the public against us too, Amish and non-Amish alike.

None of these people is or has ever been Amish. That doesn't surprise you, does it? But don't worry, that doesn't stop them from telling the world exactly what the Amish believe, as if they actually knew.

What the Amish believe, according to Haverstick and her posse, is that *Amish Mafia* really sucks and those of us connected with the program suck even worse. Mind you, no actual Amish people are saying any of this—just these self-appointed Amish spokespeople. When it comes to instant character assassination, they make my mother's stitch-and-bitch ladies seem like amateur gossips.

The chamber of commerce, with an "us, too" from the visitors bureau, sent around a notice to their members—three thousand Lancaster-area businesses, they said—asking them not to cooperate with the TV crews who are shooting *Amish Mafia*, *Breaking Amish*, *Return to Amish* or any similar shows.

"Whatever short-term economic impact these shows may bring, it's taking what has been a well-respected culture in our community and turning it into a fad," chamber president Baldrige said. "Whatever arguable increase in tourism may result from these shows, it is unquestionably short-term and will fade out over time and not serve our community well." Tourism dollars generate $363 million in tax revenue and support twenty-four thousand jobs, added visitors bureau spokesman Joel Cliff.

And the bashing had only begun.

Shows like ours are "bigoted and prejudiced" against the Amish, Haverstick told our local cable channel, News-11. "If it was just one of these projects and we had lots of other good films on Amish and Mennonites, it would be one thing. But we don't have other things happening but this. This is it."

Haverstick trotted out Lark McCarley, who runs the Lovelace Manor Bed and Breakfast in Lancaster. Apparently, she didn't claim the shows had hurt her business—how could she? Business was booming all over town, in part because of all the interest we had generated. But she said the tourists who'd been coming to her place lately, they were—well, they were *different*.

"I try to tell them more about the true Amish culture, what it's really like," the B & B woman said, "but whether or not they're receptive . . ." She let the thought drift off sadly.

"Today," she said, "it's like at the breakfast table, they're saying, 'Okay, we want to go see Lebanon Levi.'"

Imagine that!

Gosh, I wish I'd known they wanted to say hello. I'd have been happy to stop by.

I understand. People have a right to their opinions, whether they agree with mine or not. Programs like ours will always be controversial. We're giving people something they're not used to, and politicians, especially at election time, will ride whatever bandwagons they can find. A few years ago, New Jersey governor Chris Christie was railing against MTV's popular *Jersey Shore*, which followed the beach-house high jinks of some tacky, tanned and tattooed twentysomethings. US senator Joe Manchin of West Virginia launched a crusade against *Buckwild*, a reality show about a group of rural halfwits in the Charleston area. The show ended quickly, but only because one of its central figures, Shain Gandee, was killed in a freak carbon-monoxide accident. Oddly, Louisiana governor Bobby Jindal has embraced the cast of *Duck Dynasty*, which features some similarly colorful characters from his state.

Francis Ford Coppola certainly understood this phenomenon. More than four decades ago, he made one of the greatest movies ever, *The Godfather*. The film got slammed by touchy Italian-

American advocacy groups, who claimed the film reflected poorly on Italian-Americans. Coppola had a pretty good answer, I thought. He replied to critics by saying, "The real day-to-day reality of the Italian family that was put into the gangster film was based on my family and what I remember as a kid. You can't make films without them being personal to some extent." Of course, *The Godfather* busted box-office records, spun off two sequels and won huge critical acclaim. It's definitely the number one all-time favorite of most of the Italian-Americans I know. Like Coppola said about *The God-father*, *Amish Mafia* is personal to some of us. Forty years from now, maybe they'll put up a statue of me in downtown Lancaster—but, no, I'm not counting on it.

I'm sorry, but some of these official reactions to our show have been just plain dumb. The US Patent & Trademark Office actually refused to grant Discovery Channel a federal trademark for the term *Amish Mafia* for the TV show. The trademark examiner, Kim Moninghoff, called the name "disparaging to members of the Amish religious sect."

Honestly, where do Washington bureaucrats get off telling Americans, Amish or otherwise, what is and isn't disparaging to them or anyone else? The decision, which Discovery appealed, came from an office that had already okayed *Dutch Mafia*, *American Mafia*, *Portuguese Mafia*, *Lesbian Mafia*, *Mexican Mafia* and *Mafia Grannies*. Somehow, grandmothers are still loved by children everywhere, and all those other groups can still go outside with their heads held high.

I have a plain answer for all this: If these people don't like *Amish Mafia*, why don't they just change the channel? Or better yet, why not just turn off their televisions? The bishops would be thrilled, I'm sure, to hear they weren't watching any TV at all.

I liked what one of my Amish cousins said in the York County Blog. First, he admitted he hadn't seen the show. "I just have what I hear," he said. "And I'm not here to talk against Levi. For all I know, things might have gone way out from what he expected." Who knows? He said, "The rest of the world" might be getting an inaccurate picture of Amish culture, but "if it's not the truth, then it shouldn't offend us."

Our local businesspeople seemed to be genuinely worried. Who knew how the tourists might react? They might stop believing in the Amish fairy tale! They might start asking questions at the breakfast table! Really, anything was possible. A lot of money was made off the old story.

As the controversy raged on, Mary Haverstick called a public forum at Lancaster's First Presbyterian Church. According to the media reports, a decent-sized crowd showed up, sixty or seventy people in all. Haverstick used her made-up word *Amish-sploitation* a lot, but when she asked the audience how many had actually seen our show, only about one-third of the people raised their hands. Most of the people in the audience were dependent on whatever they were hearing—mostly from her—and on local TV and social media.

The Amish, Haverstick went on, "give us something in Lancaster. They give us a peaceful, beautiful, serene and pastoral vision. A simple lifestyle, a lesson in simplicity." They deserve "good neighborship" from the non-Amish, she said. "Our neighbors, I think, are under a certain assault."

Professor Kraybill wasn't at the meeting at the Presbyterian church, but he was mentioned prominently. Apparently, he disapproved of *Amish Mafia* every bit as much as Mary Haverstick did.

"*Amish Mafia* is a deliberate misrepresentation of their religion," Kraybill said in one of his many media interviews attacking us. "There is no shame in it for them."

The Amish hate the show too, the professor assured anyone who would listen. Did he have any polls to support his harsh assertion? As an esteemed college professor—*Dr.* Kraybill—had he conducted any academic research about the show? Well, um, no, but he said he had spoken with unnamed "Amish friends."

"When I've spoken about this program with Amish friends, they've just kind of laughed and said they never heard of this kind of thing," Kraybill told one reporter. "It's just sort of an example of the foolishness and stupidity and lies—misrepresentations I should say—that are promoted in television."

I didn't know much about Professor Kraybill. No actual Amish person had ever mentioned him to me, but when I looked him up, I understood why he sounded so distressed: He had published many, many books celebrating the sanitized Amish. Of course he responded to our show as if it were a threat. I'm sure he won't like my book either—or anyone else's that punctures the old Amish fairy tale.

Mary Haverstick's meeting got some attention around our part of Pennsylvania. There was some conversation I heard in the coffee shops and bars. The meeting was written up in the Lancaster and Harrisburg newspapers and discussed in the local news blogs, but as this public discussion got rolling, something surprising occurred. Most people rejected the dire handwringing, and they strongly supported us.

"These people in the capital wasted taxpayer money writing up a statement of petition?'" one commenter asked. Another writer, sick of politicians' pandering for votes, said, "Please, stick to what you know, BRIBES, FRACKING, KICKBACKS and PERKS!"

"So what?" asked one viewer. "I want to see if Levi is going to get it on with Esther!"

"Ok, you say Levi is ruining the Amish, but there are stores in Lancaster selling Amish stuff, Amish tours, Amish food. Maybe they should be shut down, too. It's the same thing, too."

I got a big smile from some of the locals who supported the show. Leslie Shenk from Lititz, Pennsylvania, commented on an editorial in the Lancaster newspaper: "Mary Haverstick and Lancaster Newspapers do not speak for all of Lancaster County. I for one watch and enjoy the show very much. While it is obvious some parts of the show are done for ratings, there are other aspects that those of us who live here have known about for ages. Amish Mafia does bring tourism, which is a good thing, anything that draws people here to visit is a good thing. So, if you don't like the show, don't watch it. Meanwhile, I intend to continue enjoying it." And a reader named Laurie nailed it when she said, "*Shahs of Sunset, Russian Dolls, Mob Wives* . . . just a few ethnic-centered reality shows. Amish puppy mills, abused Amish horses, kids, wives . . . REALITY that the commercializations/tourist industry here does not want to expose."

Someone else wrote: "Lebanon Levi for governor!" I think I'll take a pass on that one, but thanks for the thought.

It wasn't TV shows that were exploiting the Amish, several people said. It was local businesspeople. The people behind the tourism industry were the ones, Jeff Bender wrote to the website LancasterOnline, who were treating the Amish like animals in a zoo.

"Every day," he said, "I travel the roads here and witness peo-

ple in cars and buses stopping, staring, gawking and photographing
Amish people as they go about their daily lives. You might think they
were animals of some odd nature, with all the fuss made by the tourists . . . . It's highly disrespectful and shameful to submit any people
or group to this kind of scrutiny. But I guess the almighty dollar
trumps even human dignity."

Mostly, I tried to ignore the uproar. I went about my business,
going to work every morning with my brother Chris. I prepared for
the next TV season. I spent time with my family and friends. When
people came up and said things to me—a few were negative, far
more were positive—I always tried to be friendly with them. Clearly,
the public had spoken. They'd given a cold shoulder to the complainers and a warm embrace to us. The overwhelming majority of
the people seemed to side with me and not the governor and his
last-ditch attempt to win the hearts of Pennsylvanians.

I wasn't so worried about Mary Haverstick, her Amish-
sploitation committee, or professor Donald Kraybill. I knew that
soon enough, people would grow tired of them. I didn't care about
the chamber of commerce people and the visitors bureau people,
although some of their members are friends of mine. The misguided
business-promotion bureaucrats really weren't worth my attention
or my time. People were so glued to the TV show, hardly anyone was
listening to them, anyway.

But what about Tom Corbett? He was, after all, the governor of
Pennsylvania, and he was running for reelection. Did we really want
someone like him messing around in our business for another four
years?

Now, there was a target my size!

I hadn't gone looking for this fight. He'd come after me. When people asked me what I thought about the *Amish Mafia* backlash, it was always the governor they mentioned first. After all I'd been through so far, I decided I couldn't just ignore this Corbett guy anymore.

I'm not usually very political, but I decided this was one election I couldn't sit out.

I started talking to my friends and neighbors. I pulled my mother aside before her quilters came by. I got my brothers and sisters, stepbrothers and stepsisters involved. When Governor Corbett came to Lancaster Airport on a campaign stop, I went to his speech to meet him.

I wanted to know why he was so comfortable trashing me and the other cast members. I wanted to ask him how he knew what was in our hearts. I was eager to hear what he knew about the realities of living Amish. When did he become such an expert? I suspected he had no idea what kind of lives we led. I'm not sure he'd ever even seen the show. I thought it was time we spoke face-to-face, man-to-man. I wanted to ask why he had such a problem with our little TV show.

We never got to speak. His security guards made sure of that. The governor's lackeys were firmly planted between him and me. I guess they were nervous I might ask the governor a question, and he wouldn't know what to say.

This was all new to me, being involved in an election campaign, but I kinda took to it. This whole thing reminded me of a story I had heard about Vice President Dan Quayle. As George Bush's running mate in the 1992 presidential election, Quayle attacked the very popular Murphy Brown, a television character who—shock! shock!—was a single mom. People thought he was a dope. He lost the race, and deserved to.

I urged everyone I ran across to be sure they were registered to vote. For those who weren't, I told them how to register. For those who were, I reminded them to vote. "We have to get *him* out of office," I said. "He's a total disaster."

I didn't even have to say *Tom Corbett*. Everyone knew who I meant.

It turned out that the candidate running against the governor was actually a pretty good guy. Tom Wolf is his name. I don't generally like many politicians, because in my experience, you can't trust what they'll do once they get into office. But Wolf seemed fairly honest, and he was an undeniable improvement over Corbett.

For one thing, he wasn't building his whole campaign on attacking a cable TV show. He spoke about actual issues like the economy, getting jobs for people and paying for health care.

Some people warned me that getting into politics might be dangerous. They said, "You don't want to land on the bad side of the governor." They said, "You never know what kind of power he has." They said, "He might target you and your family."

I wasn't swayed by any of that. I was already on the bad side of the governor, and whatever power he had, he had. He'd already targeted me. Even if the new guy wasn't perfect, he had to be better than this blowhard.

It's always hard to beat an incumbent politician, people who know the political world kept warning me. Governors who are finishing their first terms tend to get elected to second terms. That's usually the way it goes.

"We'll see," I said.

Election Day was Tuesday, November 4. When the people had finally voted and the polls were closed for the night, I didn't know what to expect at all.

The election results started trickling in.

I prepared myself for a long, tense night.

To my surprise, the television news people declared a winner almost instantly. They announced the election result in a matter of minutes after the polls had closed. Governor Corbett got creamed.

Tom Wolf got nearly 55 percent of the vote, beating Corbett by almost ten full percentage points. That's a huge, humiliating defeat for a sitting governor.

I can't claim my friends and I are the ones who made the difference because that's a big spread. I will say this much—we made the margin significantly larger.

I could have warned the governor about some of this—I would have been happy to—if he'd have been willing to call his bodyguards off long enough for us to speak.

But he didn't, and he lost, and I know part of the reason why.

Don't mess with *Amish Mafia,* and don't mess with Levi.

ACKNOWLEDGMENTS

First, as always, thanks to God for sharing His love, helping to guide me down the right path and protecting me always. Now back to earth. There's a reason Amish families are so large. It takes a lot of us to watch one another's backs. I have been blessed with an amazingly loving and supportive family, Stoltzfuses and Peacheys both, starting with my late father, Eli, my mother, Mary, and my father, David. Thank you, thank you and thank you. My deepest appreciation also goes to all my brothers and sisters, and I do mean *all*: Samuel, Sadie, Katie, Mary, Henry and Christian Stoltzfus and Naomi, Rebecca, Sylvia, Mary, Esther, Daniel, John and Nancy Peachey. You guys have always been there for me. Special thanks to two other family members I love with all my heart and soul.

I am lucky to have world-class friends, Amish and English. For their own protection, I won't name them here. You know who you are. We have loved one another and trusted one another. We have led each other into occasional heaps of trouble and fun. Here's hoping that never changes.

ACKNOWLEDGMENTS

I did not wake up one day and say: "I should write the Amish book no one has ever dared to." *Amish Confidential* bubbled up gradually and with lots of help. Big thanks to all my coconspirators: To Todd Shill and Kevin Gold at Rhoads & Sinon LLP, brilliant lawyers and so much more—career advisers, business managers and true friends. To Eric and Shannon Evangelista and the super-talented crew at Hot Snakes Media, who somehow delivered a camera-shy Amish guy to millions of living rooms around the world. To Matthew Kelly, Dolores Gavin and all the other pros at Discovery Channel, who've taken a lot of heat for us and never bent once. To Anthony Mattero and Peter McGuigan at Foundry Literary + Media, who took my book dreams seriously. To Jeremie Ruby-Strauss, Louise Burke, Jennifer Berg-strom and Jennifer Robinson at Simon & Schuster's Gallery Books, who understood that Amish fans and *Amish Mafia* fans also love to read. To the Henican lit posse, James Gregorio, Janis Spidel, Larry Kramer and Roberta Teer, who made the book so much better. To Ellis Henican, my storytelling partner in crime, who can make you care about anyone, including me and my least favorite ex-governor.

Covering the Amish is one of American journalism's toughest beats. Many of the anecdotes and incidents described in this book rely on wonderful prior reporting by the talented writers, report-ers and producers at *Mennonite World Review*, the *Budget*, *Amish Country News*, *Die Botschaft*, *Legal Affairs*, *Rolling Stone*, *Phila-delphia* magazine, *Rodeo News*, the *Intelligencer Journal*, Lan-casterOnline, the *Patriot-News*, PennLive, the *Reading Eagle*, the *Indianapolis Star*, the *Blade* (Toledo), the *Hannibal Courier-Post*, the *Philadelphia Inquirer*, *USA Today*, the *New York Times*, Al Jazeera America, *Dateline*, and others. They and others have done inspiring work under impossible circumstances.

ACKNOWLEDGMENTS

One last note of appreciation: To the noble Amish of America and to those who visit Amish Country to see for themselves. All of you are seekers of the righteous. You also understand: Truth is a journey, not a destination. See you on the back roads!